To Kam

JOURNEY OF A DREAM

CONQUERING A DREAM UNDER PRESSURE

TWANY BECKHAM

IVISION PRESS, LLC

JOURNEY OF A DREAM

Copyright © 2021 by Twany Beckham

Cover Design by Mandy Morreale

Edits by Thomas Strause and Nancy Tyree

ISBN 978-0-615-84596-8

Published by IVISION PRESS, LLC

Printed in the United States

Dedication

I dedicate this book to my mother, my brothers, my family, the Whitaker family, the Berry family, the Gowers family, my closest friends (B4Ls), my mentors, my basketball coaches, my teammates, my teachers, and everyone else who believed in me throughout my life.

Table of Contents

God will never leave you empty handed. He will replace everything that you've lost. If he asks you to put something down, it's because he wants you to pick up something greater.

-Unknown

"Trust in the Lord with all your heart, and lean not on your own understanding. In all your ways acknowledge Him, and He will make your path straight."

-Proverbs 3:5-6

Foreword

By: John Calipari

There are moments in every coach's career when he looks back and reflects on some of the accomplishments throughout his career. I've been fortunate to experience so many of them, and I'm blessed to carry around an unbelievable pride for some of those moments. One of those prized memories that will forever stand out for me is seeing Twany Beckham walk across that stage and get his college degree.

If you have an understanding of where Twany has come from, how far that journey has been, the adversity he's faced along the way, the challenges he's overcome, and the trust and faith he's placed in other people to help him grow, it makes the story even more amazing.

Twany was a part of our national championship team in a limited on-court role, but he played a major part in preparing us for our special run. His contributions to that team were more valuable than most people know. Our team grew as he grew, and vice versa. Twany influenced our young players every day to work harder, spend more time in the gym and to be more committed. He did it without playing a lot, which showed me Twany's true character and dedication.

His lifelong dream was to play basketball at the University of Kentucky, and I'm so happy that he not only had that opportunity, but had the enjoyment of experiencing some special things that went on here. One of the proudest moments I had during a humbling year in our 2012-13 season was getting to hug Twany after he got to check in during the Mississippi State game. He had worked so hard to come back from a disappointing back injury, and though the appearance was for just a few seconds, it was a moment he and I will both remember for a long time. I would like to think that as Twany walked on to that court during his "Senior Day" moment that it hit him what this is all about.

At Kentucky, we talk a lot about sending players to the NBA and putting a degree in their hands. We like to call it the "Success Rate" here. When a young man comes to UK, he is either going pro, getting a degree or doing both. But it's even more than that. If all we have taught them and prepared them for is to be a first-round draft pick, we have failed them. Our goal here is to prepare these kids for the ups and downs of life, to be graceful in the face of adversity and to be humble amid success. Twany is prepared for the next step in life.

Yes, Twany is one of our 10 players who have graduated over the last four years, but he's also one of the many who came to Kentucky as a big kid and left as a young man ready to take on the world. His goal was to play for the University of Kentucky, and he fulfilled that, but he's left here with even grander dreams, higher aspirations and new goals to achieve.

As you read his story, I think you will grow to respect

him even more as I have throughout his two-and-a-half years at Kentucky. He is a national champion, a graduate of the University of Kentucky, but even more importantly, a fine young man. I couldn't be prouder of how far he's come.

Chapter 1:
I WEATHERED THE STORM

I was driving on I-64 East heading toward Lexington, Kentucky, in one of the largest snow storms I had ever seen. Cars were pulled over to the side of the road with their hazard lights flashing due to the terrible visibility conditions. Throughout the drive I encountered numerous wrecks, most likely due to the slick conditions on the road. I had one mission on my mind, get to Lexington as fast as I could. I was not worried about the snow or ice on the road; my mind was completely focused on getting to the University of Kentucky Men's Basketball Office to meet with Head Coach John Calipari. During the whole drive, all that I could think about was how I would react when meeting Coach Calipari for the first time. I thought about the things that I would say and those that I would not, but at the end of the day I wanted to present myself as I truly am.

Before that day I had only been to Lexington a few other times so I had no clue where I was going and the weather conditions were not making navigating any easier. Due to the snow I was running late, but I had to drive the speed limit because of the weather. This was the most nervous hour-and-fifteen-minute drive that I had ever made in my life. I remember calling my mom as I was getting off the exit and her saying, "Don't be nervous; be yourself and everything should work out." My mom and I hardly ever pray on the phone together, but for some odd reason we said a short prayer. Before I knew it, I was pulling into the Joe Craft Center parking lot with my dreams on the line.

As soon as I arrived at the Craft Center, I called Coach Kenny Payne who then met me at the front of the Craft Center. I was so nervous that I could feel my legs shaking as I walked. I was surprised Coach Payne did not call me out on how nervous I was because when I shook his hand I was shaking so hard that he may have thought I had something wrong with me. Coach Payne made me feel welcome and led me in the direction of Coach Calipari's office. Coach Payne and I sat down at Coach Cal's desk and started conversing about the drive that I had just endured and some small basketball talk. Coach Payne informed me that he had played at the University of Louisville so I felt that I had an automatic connection to him because I was from Louisville. I always thought that it would be weird to be from Louisville and play or coach at the University of Kentucky because of the deep rivalry that exists between each of the two schools.

Before I knew it, I was shaking the hand of the coach that I had dreamed about playing for. I admired him so much because of how well his teams played and the success that he has had with his point guards. Coach Calipari calmly walked into his office and sat down at his desk. In one hand he had his coffee, and in the other he had a folder with a bunch of paper work. I thought, "Wow, I'm finally in front of Coach Calipari" and realized that this moment could change my life. I was trying my hardest to hide how nervous I was. I continuously wiped the palms of my hands on my dress pants and sat up in the chair with the best posture that I could. I tried to hide my smile and excitement and tried to remain as serious as the situation at hand was. He looked as calm as could be, just as if it were another day at work. Once I noticed that Coach Calipari was just another human being, my nerves started to fade. It was kind of like being nervous before a big-time basketball game, but as soon as the ball is tipped the nerves go away. At this point my nerves were out the window and I was sitting in the chair directly across from Coach Calipari as confident as I could be.

Kenny Payne and I had held many phone conversations about me transferring to UK, but now it was time to discuss this opportunity with Coach Calipari. My mission had changed from surviving the snowstorm to becoming a member of the University of Kentucky men's basketball team. I did not expect our meeting to last very long because I assumed Coach Calipari would be short on time. I knew that I only had about three or four minutes to make my dream a reality.

I was prepared to inform Coach Calipari of how badly I wanted to become a Kentucky Wildcat and how I could be a great attribute to the team, but to my surprise I didn't have to do too much convincing. After meeting for about fifteen minutes, Coach Calipari agreed for me to join the team under a few guidelines. He offered me a walk-on spot and I had to promise to keep my grades at a respectable level and to keep my nose clean and out of trouble. My eyes lit up like a light bulb and I felt like I had just been drafted to the NBA. My dream had finally become a reality and I was ready to prove the world wrong. Coach Calipari stressed to me that this program is not for everybody and that this would probably be the hardest thing that I had ever gone through in my life. He also informed me to look forward to no playing time and any playing time that I would see would be the result of hard work and dedication. This was right up my alley. I am a fighter at heart and someone who works hard to accomplish what I want. I may not have always been the most talented guy, but my hard work has gotten me to where I am today in both basketball and in life. I stood up and shook hands with Coach Calipari and hugged Coach Payne. I needed to drive back home immediately to pack up. The winter term was scheduled to begin the next day.

Immediately after the meeting, I called my mom and

told her the good news. She was ecstatic. God had heard the prayer we had made before the meeting. On the drive home my phone blew up from reporters and local news stations about me being the new addition to the UK men's basketball roster. How word traveled that fast is still a mystery to me to this day. I hadn't told a single soul except my mom and somehow it seemed like the whole state of Kentucky already knew. During the entire drive home in the snowstorm, I was on the phone smiling and answering questions from local reporters. My friends who keep up with UK basketball began calling shocked about the news that they were reading online. A lot of them could not believe the news and thought that they were seeing misprints. Family members started calling and placing their bids for tickets, especially for the Louisville game. I was already getting a taste of the fame that comes along with being a UK basketball player. I could tell I was about to be introduced to a whole new lifestyle.

***

Chapter 2:
MAMA WAS THE ROCK

Have you ever gone to sleep at night not knowing whether the electricity will be on when you wake up in the morning? Have you ever woken up in the morning feeling scared because you didn't know if someone had broken into your house throughout the night? Have you ever woken up in the morning and had to get two other individuals ready for school because your mom was already at her first job and your dad was not around? Growing up in these circumstances I never imagined my life could have turned out the way it has.

I grew up on 10th and Muhammad Ali Blvd in Beecher Terrace, one of the toughest projects in the downtown area of Louisville, Kentucky. There were only two ways of making it out of the hood, going to school or going to prison. Around the same time I was growing up in Beecher Terrace, other projects around the city were getting torn down. The residents of those projects were forced to move into our projects, which created a situation where groups of people who did not like each other were all living in the same small area. Violence was inevitable. I never knew which family member or friend was going to fall victim to it.

From the day I was born, Mom said she knew that I was going to be a basketball player. I was a long and slender infant, had really big hands, and was always very bouncy. It only took about four years of my life until others began to see in me what my mom had seen in me since birth. I was tall for my age and basketball came natural to me. I can remember going to the parks and watching the old heads from the neighborhoods play basketball. Several times my mom had to chase after me as I interrupted the game by running all over the court. Sometimes my mom even had to spank me to get me off the court. What four-year-old kid do you know would run on the court and try to play with the old men? Already at this point in my life, my name and basketball were associated with one another. I was this little snotty nosed kid whom everybody called Twany known for running around the projects with a basketball always in his hand.

My mom would get nervous when I was out of the house for long periods of time, but she knew I wouldn't be happy if I couldn't play basketball all hours of the day. She ended up buying miniature basketball goals and placed them in the apartment so I could play basketball and she could keep a closer eye on me.

Everyone in the family always praised me for my talents and how advanced I was at such a young age. My mom always credited my dad for my basketball talents, but I never believed her. At the time, I didn't know my dad so I couldn't compare my talents with his. Because of this, I always credit my mom for my basketball talents. I used to joke with my mom all the time and call her Lisa Leslie because she is dark skin, tall and could play a little ball.

Growing up in this part of town was good and bad for me. There were kids in the neighborhood who were all about sports just like I was, but then there were also kids who were always fighting and always looking to get into some kind of trouble. I ran with a group of kids that are still my closest friends to this day. Jazz, Eddie, Leroy, Quan, and Wan were my friends, but we all considered our bond to be like a brotherhood. Basketball is what initially formed our bond, but we grew to love each other like brothers. Quan and Wan's dad, Dave, was the first basketball coach any of us had. Dave worked at the community center in Beecher Terrace called Baxter and coached a basketball team for our age group. We were all seven years old when we first started playing for Dave. We played teams from other projects' community centers. Each and every year we managed to win the league championship for our age group. Coach Willie, who coached the older kids from our community center, would also make me play with his team. There would be times when I didn't think I could adjust to playing with the older kids, but Coach Willie gave me no choice. My talent level was far beyond my age and Coach Willie was one of the first people to truly realize my potential. Having a community center like Baxter and having Dave and Willie as positive role models kept a lot of kids around the neighborhood out of trouble.

My mom really liked the basketball league and liked the friends I was making. Unfortunately, it was only a matter of time before I was pulled into the mix with the bad kids. It was easier to get pulled with the bad kids due to the fact that there were more of them. Sometimes as a kid growing up in the projects, I felt that I had to show some toughness or kids would run all over me. I can remember getting into fights because other kids would try to start trouble for no reason or act like bullies because they were bigger or older. My mom did not raise me to be a fighter, but there was no way I could let kids run all over me. The worst thing that could happen to a kid living in the projects was getting the reputation of being a punk or labeled as soft. I had won a couple fights and started bullying other kids. I was following the older kids in the neighborhood and began going down the wrong path.

This was not the kid that I wanted to grow up to be. I had two younger brothers that looked up to me and I was not being a good role model for them. My two younger brothers and I are really close in age. We are all one year apart and all have different dads. We had no choice but to be close and my mom made sure of that. She treated us all the same and didn't give any one of us more attention than the other. My mom was one who believed in separate but equal. She wouldn't buy me a shirt without buying my two younger brothers a shirt. I couldn't get a snack out of the cabinet without my brothers getting a snack. I can remember a lot of times for Christmas that my brothers and I would all get the same number of gifts. The only advantage that I had being the oldest child was that in our three-bedroom apartment I got my own room and my twoyounger brothers had to share.

Even though my brothers and I were close, we had a lot of fights while mom was at work. This may be where my competitive nature comes from. My brothers and I would fight about anything and everything. These fights weren't any girly fights. These fights were all out, trying to break each other's necks type fights. Most of our fights were over video games. One brother would brag about winning and the other brother would be pissed off about it.

We have that fighter mentality instilled in us from our mom. Mom had no choice but to be a strong woman. At the age of 13 she was kicked out of her mom's house and forced to find a way on her own. She went house to house for a while before settling in with a good friend of hers. She stopped going to school her 12th grade year and started working, but she eventually went back and earned her GED. When my mom was 18 she gave birth to me, and by the age of 21 she was a single parent with three boys. Growing up I can always remember mom working two jobs to provide food and clothing for us. I can't recall our dads consistently being there other than giving mom money for birthday and Christmas presents. My dad not being in my life affected me to some degree, but not as much as one would think. I give all that credit to my mom. Any support that I needed, she was there. My brothers' dads were around a little more than mine and they would include me in everything. I always appreciated this mainly because it showed that they cared about me too.

As we got older, my brothers and I each took different paths in life. My second youngest brother Andre and I seemed to be on the same path at first. Growing up we played on the same football and basketball teams. Andre was a great football player and played basketball in the winter to pass time. However, Andre never took school seriously and as far as I can remember never had the dream of playing sports in college. I almost believe that Andre played sports just because I did. He probably noticed the attention that everyone gave me because of my success in athletics and he might have wanted the same treatment.

It was good having a brother like Andre because he pushed me. He was my biggest competitor, my biggest critic, but also one of my biggest fans. In high school basketball practices, he would be the one trying to guard me all practice. In really tough competitive drills I was always matched up against my brother.

My youngest brother Mark fell victim to the violence and negativity of the projects. He has been in and out of jail throughout my life. Mark being locked up so much has forced him to miss so much time with our family. Family functions didn't feel complete without him being there. Throughout most of my career, Mark was not able to attend games or events with the rest of the family. No matter how much success I was having, Mark not being there through it all took some degree of happiness away. Mark really wasn't a troubled kid; he was just easily influenced.

I didn't start out perfect by any means either. I had my fair share of problems. I went through a phase where I was talking back to mom and fighting other kids in the neighborhood. At the time, I could care less about school. I caused a lot of trouble in the classroom. I didn't mind teachers and talked back to them all the time. When I was in elementary school, Mom used to take me to school and as soon as she left I would run out of the building. One time I attempted it and Mom outsmarted me. She circled the school grounds and caught me walking away from the building. She took me to the Home of the Innocence, a place where troubled kids are detained. At first, I tried to act tough but when she started leaving out the door I cried and she came back and got me.

When mom would cook dinner, I used to complain about her touching my food while fixing my plate. One day mom got fed up with it and told me if she couldn't touch my food then I wasn't going to eat. Well words were exchanged and I found myself packing a bag to move out. I probably said some things to mom that I should not have said. Mom was fed up with my behavior and decided to kick me out of the house. I was only in middle school and I remember her telling me that if I'm not going to mind her I needed to find another place to live. At that time, I acted like it didn't bother me and I packed my bag as if I was happy to be moving out. The only problem with the situation was I was packing a bag but with nowhere to go. I called my older cousin, Dion Lee, and asked if I could stay with him for a little while. He agreed and picked me up soon after. The whole two weeks I was gone I missed my mom like crazy. It was cool to live with my cousin Dion but there was nothing like being comfortable in your own house. My mom didn't call me at all the whole time I was gone but I knew deep down she was missing me too. I eventually called her and apologized and she allowed me to move back into the house. I had no intentions to ever talk back to mom again because now I knew she meant business and wasn't going to let any of her sons run over her. Mom had basically provided everything for me and I learned that I needed to be more appreciative of her.

I used to hang out a lot with my cousin Tywain. Tywain was a few years older than I was and I looked up to him a lot. We were always together and it was rare to see one of us without the other. One night that I wasn't with him he was shot and killed. When I received the news, I was crushed. It was the first time in my young life that I had lost someone really close to me. Death had hit really close to home. I saw how badly the death of my cousin affected my family and my auntie. Losing a child had to be tough for one to endure. My auntie was such a great lady and no way did she deserve to lose her son. My mom worked so hard to make sure my brothers and I stayed on the right track and out of trouble. Sometimes bad things happen to good people and we as humans cannot control that. It took me quite some time to get over losing Tywain. I was young and didn't know how to deal with having someone close to you pass away. With the death of my cousin always on my mind, it pushed me to become more focused because I know that is what he would have wanted me to do. I immediately dedicated all my time to my basketball career because at the time I thought it was my only way out of the projects and my only hope for a better life.

***

Chapter 3:
A SECOND CHANCE

My troublesome childhood followed me into my freshman year at the prestigious Ballard High School. I still could not get my life together. I was doing the same things that I had been doing my whole life. I acted up in class, did not care about my school work, and did not get along with my coaches. I was very fortunate to be playing for coaches who really cared about me and wanted to see me do well because with my behavior and attitude I should have never made the team.

Ballard's varsity head coach, Chris Renner, followed me a lot throughout my last season of middle school basketball. At that time, having Coach Renner come to your games to evaluate you to me was like having Kentucky at your games.

Ballard is one of the best high school basketball programs in the state of Kentucky and it is very hard to make their team. It was very exciting because three of my friends from my neighborhood were also going to Ballard to play basketball. However, my freshman year was a disappointment. I was the best freshman that Coach Renner had brought in that year. I should have been the starting point guard on the varsity team as a freshman, but I did not have the mentality to fill that role.

My mentality was to fit in with the other freshman kids and be a class clown. I was still struggling to make basketball my main priority and that caused me to have a terrible start to my freshman season. What the coaches saw in me, I did not see in myself. I started out dressing varsity, but was slowly demoted to junior varsity and right after that I found myself riding the bench for the freshman team. For everybody who watched me play in middle school, my family, and my friends, this was embarrassing. However, at the time I did not care one bit. My terrible play and bad attitude was a cancer to the freshman team and I found myself kicked off and in the principal's office asking for a release. Chris Huff, who was the freshman coach, was a big supporter of my abilities and we had a great relationship. Coach Huff kicking me off the freshman team said a lot about how poor my actions were at that time. The news had spread around the high school halls that I would possibly be transferring and my friends were not pleased about what they had heard. My brother Andre, who was in the 8th grade at the time, was also planning on attending Ballard to play basketball with me. He was not happy about the decision I was making.

At this point in my life I did not care about anybody's feelings except my own. I was acting extremely selfish. The night after I spoke with the Ballard's principal the junior varsity coach, Coach Ray Klein, gave me a call. He offered me my position back on the junior varsity team as long as I could agree to be a good teammate, have a positive attitude, and stay out of trouble in the classroom. For a young man with no direction in life, I had to make an important decision. I had a long talk with my brother and promised him that I would be at Ballard the next year so that he and I could play together. I called Coach Klein back and agreed to rejoin the team under his terms.

Coach Klein held junior varsity practice a couple days after our phone conversation. He sat the team down and introduced me back to the team like I was a new player. It was weird because it seemed like some players didn't want me back on the team. The only ones who looked like they wanted me to be part of the team were my close friends. It got even worse the next game that we had to play. All the parents knew I had been kicked off the freshman team. When I ran out with the junior varsity team for the next home game you could hear the whispering among the crowd of people wondering how I was back in uniform. I didn't let any of this bother me. I just stuck to the rules of Coach Klein, did what I had to do, and finished the year out strong. I ended up playing pretty well which made

Coach Renner consider letting me playing varsity in the summer.

I did not think about the significance of Coach Klein's gesture at the time, but looking back on it I am so thankful Coach Klein reached out to help me. It is funny how one random act of kindness can impact another's life so much. If Coach Klein had not reached out to me and asked me to rejoin the junior varsity team my whole life could have been different. I might have never picked up a basketball again. Without basketball keeping me in the gym instead of on the streets I would have inevitably gotten mixed up with the wrong crowd.

Life really changed for me that summer. I grew from 6 feet to 6'4" and my body started really maturing. The first day of school that fall I was walking the halls like a new person. Everyone had noticed the change. Physically I had changed a lot but it was more than that. It was something about my attitude and my persona that had people looking at me differently. I was super nice to my teachers. I was more focused on my school work. Basketball had finally become a major priority to me. My older cousin Kevin started preaching to me that for me it was the NBA or nothing. Kevin was an influence on my life because he was also chasing his dream of becoming a professional music artist. Besides my mom and brothers, Kevin was probably my biggest supporter. My relationship with Kevin was unlike any other relationship I had with anyone else. Kevin had big expectations for me and mainly wanted to see me outshine the competition. At times it seemed like Kevin wanted it for me more than I wanted it for myself. If I ever laid the basketball up during a basketball game, I knew that I was going to hear Kevin's mouth after the game. He wanted me to dunk everything and shoot every time that I touched the ball. Kevin is 5' 6" and he always said that if he had my height he would average 40 points a game. That was just his mentality. Kevin always told me that I was too nice on the basketball court and that I needed to show people no mercy.

Things with Kevin got interesting after my junior year of high school. He got into some trouble with the law and had to go prison. Up to that point Kevin hadn't missed one of my games since I was in middle school. This affected me a lot because I was losing one of my biggest supporters and more importantly, someone who always pushed me to do better. While Kevin was in prison we still maintained a close relationship. We wrote letters back and forth frequently. I drove to visit him whenever I could. I tried my hardest to keep him caught up with my basketball career but it was tough on him to not actually be there. Kevin would send me pictures of his prison cell and in the background, I could see my newspaper clippings hanging up on his wall.

***

Chapter 4:

A STAR ON THE RISE

From the beginning of my sophomore season, I started off strong and never looked back. As a sophomore, I was the starting point guard for a top ranked team in Kentucky that had 10 seniors. The point guard that had started the previous year was now a junior. I think he and the team understood that Coach Renner felt like me starting point guard was best for the team so there wasn't much controversy about it.

From my sophomore season on, Coach Renner and I built a relationship that was like no other I had ever had with a coach. I got really close to him and at the time he was one of the only male figures that I could trust with decisions regarding my life and future. His decision to start me as a sophomore showed how much confidence he had in me. Coach Renner having that confidence in me made me a much better player. I started getting notoriety around the state of Kentucky for my play on the court. There was a lot of talk around town about Ballard's 6'4" skinny kid with corn rows that could really play. I started to see more and more of my family coming out to watch me play and it felt good having people who were in my corner and at my games supporting me.

My team managed to make it to the state tournament that year. We ended up losing in the semi-finals to Pleasure Ridge Park on a buzzer beater. If we had won that game we probably would have gone on to win state. I played pretty well in our two games and attracted some interest from some small Division I colleges, but what I remember most about that state tournament was its location. It was held in Rupp Arena. I can remember running out onto the floor for the first time and telling myself that I would love to play here and one day have my jersey hanging in the rafters. I don't think that I could have made that statement to myself a few years before. This shows how much confidence I was gaining in myself. That was also when my dream to play for UK got serious. I just loved Rupp Arena.

The summer going into my junior year was a big one for me. I wanted to carry over the success that I had from my sophomore year and I wanted to come back as a much improved junior. That summer I got an invitation to join the Derek Smith All Stars AAU traveling basketball team. Kris

Vance started a traveling team in the memory of his good friend Derek Smith, who passed away in August of 1996. Years ago, while playing basketball at the University of Louisville's practice facility I met Nolan Smith, the son of Derek Smith. We became close friends throughout the years, so when I got the opportunity to play in memory of his dad I could not turn it down. There were several AAU teams that asked me to play, but I quickly decided to play with the Derek Smith All Star Team. Steve Berry was going to be the head coach of my age group. I had played on several AAU teams for Mr. Berry and during that time I developed a great relationship with Mr. and Mrs. Berry and their son, Brett.

Traveling with the team that summer created memories that I will never forget. Before joining the Derek Smith All Star Team, I had not been out of the state of Kentucky very often. I was getting the opportunity to see the world while playing basketball. I got to travel to places like Las Vegas, Orlando, and Los Angeles. As a kid coming from where I came from, those trips meant more to me than playing basketball. I was getting a chance to see the world. My only issue was that my mom and brothers could not travel and see the world with me. I did not like doing things without my mom and brothers because those were the people that had always been there through the struggles. I wanted them to be a part of any success I was having. I always reminded myself that if I ever made it to the NBA, I would make sure that my mom and brothers would have a chance to see the world. My mom was in her mid 30s and had never been out of the state of Kentucky.

Although I was being introduced to many new parts of the world, I was also introducing the world to Twany Beckham. I was playing really well at the AAU tournaments and college coaches were taking notice. My mom started receiving phone calls from college recruiters. Everything was happening so fast and my life was changing. I was getting more and more confident about myself day by day. My mom was getting notoriety for having a son that was the up and coming star of Ballard High School and around the neighborhood I was becoming known as being the next kid to make it out of the projects. Through everything that was happening, I never wanted to change who I was.

***

Chapter 5:

UNEXPECTED BLESSING

It was a mid-week day and school was letting out. We didn't have practice that afternoon and I didn't want to go straight home. I asked one of my teammates, who only lived two blocks away from Ballard, if I could go home with him for a little while to hang out and watch television. After a few hours of hanging out, I realized it was getting late and I should probably head home. I wasn't driving yet, so I had to look at the bus schedule and see what time the busses were running. On my way out to the bus stop I noticed that there was a car sitting in my friend's driveway. In the car was a white man talking to my friend's older brother. Not even two steps after I walked out of the house I heard a voice from the car yell my name. I continued to walk hoping that my name wasn't what I really heard. Once again, someone from the car yelled my name. This time the voice was louder and I turned around and looked. The white man that was sitting in the car signaled for me to come over and I just stopped and looked. When I noticed my friend's big brother was looking at me and signaled for me to come over, I realized that it was safe to walk over to the car.

When I got over to the car I leaned my head down into the window and the white guy sitting in the car asked me if I had taken the ACT. I immediately thought, "What the hell? Why is he asking me this? He doesn't even know me." I answered very rudely, "No," and the guy rambled on about why it was important for me to take the ACT early. I was very uninterested in this conversation and just kept nodding my head at everything he was saying. Everything he said went in one ear and out the other. I didn't mean to be rude, but he was a stranger to me and I just didn't know what his motives were. After a few minutes of us talking, I said that I needed to go so I didn't miss the bus. I turned and quickly walked away toward the bus stop to head home.

A few weeks into the season, Ballard was playing in the Louisville Invitational Tournament. When I was coming out of the locker room after the game, I noticed that same guy was there sitting in courtside seats. As I walked past him he noticed me and grabbed me. He said, "Hey, Beckham, you ready for the ACT?" I once again looked at him like he was crazy and just said, "No".

He said, "Son, you need to get prepared for the test and I can help you." I once again nodded my head and let it go in one ear and out the other. But something was strange about this situation; the way he looked at me and grabbed me just wasn't normal. It felt like I had some kind of relationship with this guy and I didn't even know him. I stood back from where he was sitting for about 20 minutes and just watched him. He appeared to be highly respected and everyone who walked past him stopped and spoke to him. So I began to think that maybe I should not be so rude and give him a chance.

A couple of months passed and the ACT was coming up. I knew that I needed help studying for the test and an image of this guy kept coming in my head. It was during a home game one Friday night when I saw that guy sitting in the stands. I made it a point to get in contact with him before the night was over. After the game, I ran over to him and politely introduced myself and asked him what his name was and if he would help me study for the ACT. He introduced himself as Stan Whitaker. He was really nice and agreed to help me. I had expected him to be rude and not willing to help me because of the way I had acted toward him during our two previous encounters. We exchanged phone numbers and planned on getting in contact with each other soon to set up study session times.

Stan Whitaker had been a principal in Jefferson County for many years and had also been a college professor. His passion in life was working with kids, helping kids, and attending basketball games. He and his wife, Bonnie Whitaker, loved to support kids and would do anything to help them. I later found out that one of my teammates was also starting to do ACT study sessions with Mr. Whitaker. I called Mr. Whitaker a couple of days after we officially met and set up times to meet for study sessions. However, I failed to show up to our first three study sessions. I did not mean to miss the sessions. I had problems finding a way from my house to where the study sessions were being held. The mistake I made was not calling Mr. Whitaker and explaining the difficulties I was having with arranging travel plans. I managed to make it to the fourth session. Bonnie helped with the sessions also. She worked mostly on the math part while Mr. Whitaker worked mainly on reading and writing.

Just after the first few study sessions with the Whitakers, I knew there was something that emotionally attached me to them. I had never met two people that were so nice, caring, and giving. They took time out of their busy lives to help kids that they didn't even really know.

Once again, someone reached out to me and performed a random act of kindness. The Whitakers had no obligation to help me. They simply chose to help me. They noticed I was a kid with a lot of potential and they wanted to make sure I was taking the necessary steps to ensure that I could continue an educational career after high school. I can honestly say that without the Whitakers I am not sure if I could have scored well enough on the ACT to get accepted to any college. The

Whitakers helped me get my life moving in the right direction. Without doing well on the ACT my basketball career might have ended after high school. Without college basketball being an option, I may have settled for staying in the projects of Louisville because at that time I saw basketball as being my only way out. Without this random act of kindness by the Whitakers my whole life might have been different.

My relationship with the Whitakers grew and we began spending time outside of the study sessions. I could talk to the Whitakers about anything that was going on in my life and they would listen and give me great advice. From this time forward, the Whitakers never missed a high school game of mine. I don't know how I allowed that relationship to grow so quickly. I am not one that trust people easily. I never allowed anyone besides my mom and my brothers to be in my business, but it was different with the Whitakers. Their hearts were so full of caring and giving. There were times when Mr. Whitaker would see a homeless guy walking on the side of the street and would pull over to give the guy money to eat.

I always wanted to be around Mr. Whitaker because of the conversations and fun we would have. He would tell old school jokes and have stories from back when he was a little kid that were always hysterical. The best thing about hanging out with Mr. Whitaker was watching basketball games on television, preferably UK games. He was the biggest UK fan I had ever met. Throughout the whole game he would commentate on how UK should be playing, who needed to be in the game, and what coaching decisions needed to be made. At that time Rajon Rondo, who was a good friend of both of ours, was playing for UK. Mr. Whitaker would try to coach Rondo from home on his couch. At that time, I was a really good basketball player in high school, but was only being recruited by low to mid-level schools. Sometimes watching UK games with Mr. Whitaker, I would say to him, "What do you think it would be like if I were playing for UK one day? Would you yell at the TV screen like you yell at Rondo?"

He would say, "Hell, yes! If you made a bad play, I'm telling Coach to take your ass out." He was passionate about basketball just like I was. I think that's one of the reasons why we bonded so quickly. Mr. Whitaker was like the dad I never had. I could talk to him about anything. On the weekends, I would ask Mr. Whitaker to come get me and just go to his house to relax and talk. He hardly ever said no. If he did it was because he was busy and he would always reschedule.

I was hesitant to tell my mom about the relationship that I was forming with Mr. Whitaker because I didn't know how she would react. I imagined that my mom would react negatively. I thought she would accuse Mr. Whitaker for wanting something from me and explain to me that no one is that nice for no reason. Usually I would have agreed with her, but this situation was different. I told my brothers about Mr. Whitaker and the relationship I was forming. My brothers also questioned what Mom would do if she found out. We all knew how Mom felt about my brothers and me staying close to one another, and I was worried she would think my relationship with the Whitakers would make my brothers and I grow apart.

Around this time my neighborhood was getting really bad. Robberies and murders were occurring daily. On New Year's Eve of my junior year of high school I was heading out to party with some of my friends when I witnessed a guy murdered right outside my apartment building. I knew the guy that was killed and it was extremely difficult to witness. Death was right at my doorstep. If I had left just a few seconds sooner, I could have been in the middle of the conflict and caught a stray bullet.

The day after the murder, I realized how much the incident bothered me. I was tired of living in an area where I never felt safe. I wanted to ask Mr. Whitaker if I could move in with him and Bonnie for the remainder of my high school career. I was nervous about asking him because I didn't know what he would say, but I was more nervous about how my mom would have felt about it. My mom had also had enough with the violence and found a house in south Louisville. South Louisville wasn't too much better, but it was better than the area of town we had been living in. I told Mr. Whitaker about the situation that had happened that night right outside my apartment building. He was saddened by the news and talked to me about how I needed to live in a better environment. I felt like he was hinting at having me stay with him. Ideally this was the right time to ask him if I could move in with him, but when the time came I froze up and couldn't get it out. Mr. Whitaker and I were close, but I just didn't know how he would take that question so I left it alone.

The relationship between Mr. Whitaker and myself grew more and more by the day and I began to call him Pops. It would be funny when the Whitakers and I would go out to eat at restaurants and people would ask what the relation between us was. Pops always said, "He is my son." The looks on people's faces were priceless. Pops is this older, grey haired, white guy and I am this skinny, light skinned, black haired guy with no resemblance to him at all. Pops and I would just get a kick out of people's reactions to him and me being in public together. To people who didn't know me growing up, you could not have told them differently that Mr. Whitaker was not my Pops.

I was learning a new way of life. The Whitakers taught me how to treat people with respect, how to prioritize my life, and handle responsibilities. I eventually told my mom about the relationship I had with the Whitakers and she was very accepting. Her thought was simply that if someone is willing to help change who I am for the better, she had no problem with the relationship. The only thing she asked was to meet the Whitakers. Her approval of the Whitakers was important for the relationship to continue to grow.

***

Chapter 6:

DO WHAT IS BEST FOR YOU

The 2006-2007 Kentucky High School Basketball Preseason Polls were out. Ballard was ranked number two in the state behind Scott County and I was rated as a top three player in the state. Everything was in line for Ballard to have a successful year and for me to have a great senior season. The previous three years we had been rated top three in the state and came up short of winning the state championship. This year my teammates and I felt like we had to win the state championship or our season would be a huge disappointment. We had experience along with great size and athletic ability. This was my year to prove to Division I scouts that I was capable of earning a scholarship. I was being recruited by mid-level Division I schools, but I wanted to gain the interest of high-level Division I schools.

The season started off really well. We were mid-way

through the season and had only lost one game which was to number one Scott County. We were the talk of the town. All of our games were sold out. At this time, we were King of the Bluegrass tournament champions, Louisville Invitational Champions, and third place finishers in a Christmas tournament in Ocala, Florida. I made the All-Tournament team at the King of the Bluegrass Tournament, I was MVP at the Louisville Invitational Tournament, and I also made the All-Tournament Team at the Christmas tournament in Florida.

My coach was receiving calls daily from colleges about me, but none from Kentucky. An assistant coach from Kentucky attended one of the games at the King of the Bluegrass tournament and I performed really well, but still no call from Kentucky. It became frustrating. My dream school, which was an hour down the road, wasn't taking interest in me. However, I never hung my head and continued to play really well the rest of the season. My coach and I would sit down and talk recruiting in his office all the time and he would never mention anything about Kentucky. I didn't know if he was shooting down my dreams or if he was just being realistic with me. My mindset was to keep working hard and Kentucky would call eventually. I would play well against Rondo and other professionals that would come back home during the summer, so I knew I was good enough.

Signing day was right around the corner so I had to start going on my visits. A small school in Indianapolis known as IUPUI grabbed my attention and I decided to take a visit. The coaches from IUPUI were always at my high school evaluating me and keeping in contact. I really liked their coaches and felt that they were sincere about the whole recruiting processes. My mom went with me on the visit and we enjoyed our time. I'm a city kid so I really enjoyed Indianapolis and could see myself living there for four years. On my visit I got to meet Peyton Manning and some of the other Indianapolis Colts players. They were all very complimentary of IUPUI's head basketball coach. IUPUI really wanted me and I liked that.

At the time they had a player by the name of George Hill who is currently playing in the NBA. While on my visit, George sat me down and told me about how the name on the front of the jersey didn't matter and that if you could play, the NBA would find you. George had a valid point because there are a lot of players in the NBA that came from schools I had never heard of, but in the back of my mind I've always thought wearing Kentucky across my chest meant more than anything. He was going into his junior season and he told me it would probably be his last. I wondered, "How in the world would he go into the NBA from IUPUI?" George mentioned to me that he had all the top schools in the country recruiting him coming out of high school but he decided to go somewhere he was really wanted and would be able to get the playing time he desired. All of this was making a lot of sense to me, and I started falling in love with IUPUI. Two things won me over with IUPUI. George said he would move positions and play two guard so I could play point guard. Also, IUPUI was recruiting one of my best friends from my neighborhood, Leroy Nobles.

Growing up, Leroy and I had mentioned that it would be awesome to play college basketball together and be roommates. Now it finally seemed like it could be a reality. IUPUI had everything going in their favor for me to sign with them and I felt like that was where my heart was. On the flip side of things, I knew I would get a lot of negative comments from my friends and family back at home about going to such a small school. I really cared a lot about what my friends and family thought, but my mom told me that they are not the ones who have to live with this decision-- it's me. At first, I could tell my mom was kind of skeptical about IUPUI because she had never heard of the school and she knew I had always dreamed about playing at the Kentucky's of the world. I left my visit very happy; however, I still wanted to visit a few other schools before making my decision.

A few weeks later Leroy took his visit to IUPUI and fell in love with the school and the opportunities IUPUI presented. He decided that IUPUI was where he wanted to continue his basketball career. It kind of put some pressure on me because we had always talked about experiencing college life together and here was the opportunity right in front of us. Shortly after his visit, Leroy committed. I followed and committed too. It was a bittersweet feeling because I was going to a Division I college to play basketball and earn an education, but it wasn't my dream school. Committing took weight off my shoulders and allowed me to go out and continue to play well without worrying about colleges calling anymore.

As the news spread around the city no one had anything good to say about the decision I had made. I had to answer questions daily about why I chose such a small school and it began to irritate me. I can count on one hand how many people congratulated me for my decision. As the season went on I kept hearing negative comments about IUPUI and I began to doubt my decision. It was so stressful and almost made me feel like I had done something bad. I tried to remain positive, but it was hard when so many people around me were being negative.

The situation weighed heavy on my mind and I had a couple bad games during that time. I sat down and talked to my mom and high school coach about it. Both of them told me to do what would make me happy. I didn't know if it was the negativity from others that was bringing me down or if I was truly questioning the decision myself. I started realizing that I made the decision mainly for my friend and hadn't been thinking with my best interest in mind. After long talks with my mom and my high school coach I came to the decision to part ways with IUPUI and my commitment to them. It was tough doing that because they invested so much time in me and they were planning on me to be their point guard for the future. I was happy for Leroy because I knew that he was going to get an opportunity to do his own thing and I was sure he would do very well. It was hard telling him about the decision I had made because we were close friends and I didn't want this situation to ruin us. Leroy was understanding and had nothing but respect for my decision. I told Leroy that I thought he would hate me when I decided not to go to IUPUI. He told me nothing could come between our friendship because we were like brothers.

With that situation behind me I had to refocus and prepare to finish my senior year. I got back on track and finished out the regular season 7th Region Player of the Year and headed into the post season with a lot of confidence. The post season went by like a blur and before I knew it I was getting ready for tip off of my last high school game, which was held at Rupp Arena. The only team that beat us in the state of Kentucky during the regular season was the team that was lined up across from us for the state championship game – Scott County. Twenty-four thousand people packed the arena for a high school game. I tried to imagine I was playing at Rupp Arena for a UK game.

The previous three games in the state tournament I played really well. I was hoping to do the same in the championship game. I was hoping to win over a bunch of UK fans this week by winning the state championship and being the MVP of the tournament. My plan did not go accordingly. I had the worst game of my career that night. I spent most of the game on the bench in foul trouble and could never get into rhythm while on the floor. I went one for nine from the field, but managed to grab 22 rebounds. Even with me struggling so badly, my team still found itself up eight points with four minutes left to go. I remember looking up at the scoreboard just praying those last four minutes would blow by, but those four minutes felt like they lasted a decade.

After a couple bad calls and a few turnovers, we found ourselves down in a close ball game. As the time was expiring from the clock, Scott County fans were jumping up and down and their players were hugging one another. For me, the world stopped. I just stood there in silence, tears falling from my eyes. I felt like I had blown an incredible opportunity. My brother Andre had played his heart out during the game. He was on the sideline drenched in tears. He and I both knew that game had been our last opportunity to play a sport with one another and we didn't want it to end with a loss. The clock finally reached zero and Scott County stormed the court. It almost didn't feel real. That year we didn't know what losing felt like. I wanted it so bad for my coach, my brother, and the rest of my teammates. I tried to hold back my emotions in the locker room, but it was hard sitting right next to my brother who was crying his heart out. All he kept saying was "We ain't never going to be on the same team again. I love you." My friend Eddie was just as emotional as my brother. Eddie and I used to run the neighborhood together in our Pampers and now our last game together ended in a loss. I just felt so bad for those guys. I felt like I let them down. I could have blamed my poor play on the refs calling terrible fouls on me, but no one would have wanted to hear those excuses.

Walking out of the locker room to our family and friends was the toughest part. My mom was more positive about the situation than I would have thought. Her words were "You can't win them all and I know you gave it everything you had." Her opinions about the refs were very negative, but at this point we couldn't do anything about it. My text messages on my phone all consisted of questions asking why I only scored two points in the biggest game of my life. I just ignored them and tried to stay positive. For the people who actually meant something to me, their feedback was to learn from this and move on. They told me not to hang my head because I had a great high school basketball career.

After an ending like this, I was ready for the next chapter of my life. By signing the letter of intent with IUPUI and not fulfilling my obligation to attend, the only options were prep school or junior college. When the word got out, I gained a lot of interest from prep schools and that was the route I decided to take. After my high school season was over, I visited the New Hampton School in New Hampshire and committed before my visit ended.

***

Chapter 7:

MY FIRST STOP

"Welcome to the Beautiful State of New Hampshire" the signs read as I was walking through the airport in Manchester, New Hampshire. I looked so out of place. There were no African-Americans in the airport and people were looking at me as if I were a foreigner. I was really nervous. It felt like I had just landed in a country overseas. I called my prep school coach, Pete Hutchins, to inform him that my plane had landed. Coach said he was already outside waiting for me, so I grabbed my bags and headed outside. I was anxious about getting to know him better on the 45-minute drive from the airport to the New Hampton School.

School did not start until September, but I went to school in August because I had to raise money to pay for the school's entry fee. I was given a scholarship from the school that covered tuition, but the entry fee of $1,500 was separate and I had to pay that myself. I had no idea how I was going to come up with the money. I was actually worried that Coach Hutchins would not accept me because I could not guarantee that I would be able to pay the entry fee. Thankfully, Coach Hutchins thought of an idea to solve this problem. He suggested that I come to New Hampton a month early to work and raise money for the entry fee. During that month, I worked a New Hampton basketball camp and also helped clean and paint houses around the community. I did not mind working the basketball camp, but cleaning and painting houses was very new to me. I had never done anything like this in my life. I wanted to quit and go home, but I had to keep pushing through. I would call my mom at night and complain about how I hated the work I was doing. The advice my mom gave me was "You have no choice. You have to do what you have to do. Just be thankful that someone is helping you find a way to raise the money you need." It wasn't until this conversation with my mom that I realized yet again someone was performing a random act of kindness for me. I had been so focused on how awful the manual labor work was that I had not realized I should actually be thankful for the situation. Coach Hutchins did not have to help me find a way to raise money for the entry fee, but he chose to. He gave me an opportunity to continue my basketball and educational career.

Kendall Durant, the younger cousin of Kevin Durant, was doing the exact same thing I was doing to help pay for his entry fee. This time we spent together ended up being very valuable. Kendall and I were going to be the starting guards for the team and this time we had together helped us bond and form a close relationship. Kendall, Coach Hutchins, and I were literally the only three people on campus. New Hampton was a very small community. There were no stores, no fast food restaurants, and maybe one gas station. The school was very secluded from everything. The nearest Wal-Mart was practically an hour away. I had no clue how I was going to survive. I barely had service on my cell phone. The only thing we did for fun was go to the gym and workout. It got to the point where just for fun Kendall and I would play jokes on Coach Hutchins. In the mornings when Coach Hutchins would come wake us up to get ready for work we would put chairs under the door knobs so he couldn't open the door and we would pretend like we didn't hear him knocking. Coach Hutchins used to get so mad. Several times in the morning we hid in the closets and watched him look around the room for us. Working all the way until school started allowed Kendall and me to raise the money for our entry fees and we were all set to begin school.

A couple of days before school started the rest of my teammates arrived on campus. Kendall and I were so hyped to meet our new teammates and to be around more people. The first teammate I met was Tori Gurley. He was from Rock Hill, South Carolina, and sold turkey legs for a living before applying to prep school. When I met him there was an instant connection and we decided to be roommates. He was 22 years old and was going to play both football and basketball at New Hampton. He had the personality of an old man and was really funny. I think that's why I liked him so much. He had a dream to play football for any school in the SEC, preferably South Carolina. My dream was to play for Kentucky. So, we both set a goal to at least sign with an SEC school, even if it wasn't our dream school.

The student body at New Hampton was also made up of various ethnicities. In my dorm, there were several basketball players and the rest were Asians. The Asians were some of the nicest people I had ever met. I had never had any interaction with people who come from an Asian background. They ran on a totally different schedule than most of us in the dorm. They were always up all night and cooked most of their food during the wee hours of the morning.

New Hampton was very focused on academics and this was the beginning of a new life for me. I did not have all the distractions that I had at home in Louisville. I was surrounded with all the resources and people to help me change as a person and as a student.

Once a week we had a school-wide dinner at which every student had to be dressed in formal attire. There was one problem with this whole situation – I didn't have any dress clothes in my closet so I didn't know what I was going to do. There were no clothing stores near campus so I had to borrow clothes from some of my teammates. I could remember wearing slacks that were too big, shirts that were too small, belts that were too tight, and dress shoes that were too little all just to be well prepared for the dinners. That only lasted so long. I had my mom buy me dress clothes for Christmas that year.

Basketball season was coming up and Coach Hutchins had us practicing hard so we would be in great shape for the season. I quickly noticed the advantages of going to prep school. I was practicing in front of major Division I college coaches on a daily basis. I started receiving interest from schools that never even saw me play in high school. I felt like I had made the right choice in attending prep school. Coach Hutchins did everything he could to fill our practices with coaches from the schools the players were interested in. My game was taking off and I was becoming a better player. I worked a lot on my jump shot and spent more time in the weight room. There was literally nothing else to do on campus, so I had no choice but to get better. I was labeled one of the "players to watch" in the early preseason polls.

Our season got off to a slow start. We were losing close games that we should have won. I was playing really well individually, but as a team we were struggling. This prep school league was tougher than I had anticipated. I was playing against big time guards each and every game such as Isaiah Thomas, who currently is the starting point guard for the Sacramento Kings, Dion Waiters, who currently starts for the Cleveland Cavaliers, and Anthony Crater, who was committed to play at Ohio State at the time. Each and every game I had to hold my own. There were no cupcakes. Of the prep schools we played, the majority of them had about three or four Division I players per team. I did not play against competition like this while I was at Ballard. I was finally in the light that I wanted to be in proving myself against the best in the country.

My dream had always stayed the same. I wanted to get the interest of the University of Kentucky and during one of my prep school tournaments I had the opportunity. There was a tournament being held in Boston, Massachusetts, and we played Findlay Prep out of Las Vegas. Each year Findlay Prep is rated top five in the country. This year was no different. Their point guard was DeAndre Liggins, whom Kentucky was recruiting at the time. I was hyped about this match up. In the warm ups before that game I remember being hyped and nervous at the same time. College coaches were filling the stands and more importantly I saw an assistant from Kentucky sitting courtside. My teammates knew how big this game was for me and all they kept telling me was "Let's go, Twany; this is your time." I was hiding my nervousness and was acting as confident as could be.

God must have been with me on this day. I started out making my first five shots and we got up ten points. I was not known as a great three-point shooter, but I was 4 for 4 during that game from the three-point line. Everything that could go right for me was. Every time I made a good play I tried to look over at the Kentucky coach to see if he was watching. However, DeAndre was also playing very well. He was tough to guard. Being 6'5'' I was viewed as a big point guard, but DeAndre seemed to be about 6'6''. DeAndre was a great player and I could see why Kentucky was recruiting him. As the game went on, Findlay Prep started denying me the ball and I was tiring down. They made a huge run and jumped out to a 12-point lead with about 5 minutes to go. Their size inside wore us down. We were just overmatched. We went on to lose that game, but it was the best we had played all year.

I surely thought after this game that I would get the interest of the Kentucky coaches. About a week went by and still nothing. At this point I almost decided to give up the dream of playing for Kentucky and head in a different direction, but something told me not to. Even though I hadn't heard from Kentucky, after the Findlay Prep game I gained a lot of other interest from other schools. That game let me know that I had the ability to be a big-time player and play for a big-time school. My confidence carried over into our next few games and I continued to play well along with the team. We started to win some games and got a swagger about us.

Every year the New Hampton School hosts a tournament and invites elite basketball programs. Right off the jump we were matched up with South Kent, whose starting two guards were Isaiah Thomas and Dion Waiters. Both of them were two of the top-rated guards in the country. I viewed this game as another opportunity to prove myself. I got off to another good start just like against Findlay Prep, except in this game, we had no answers for their guards. Isaiah Thomas made everything he threw up and Dion Waiters was as fierce of a player as I had ever seen. We kept it close the whole game, but never got over the edge. Isaiah Thomas finished the game with 40 points and Dion Waiters had between 20 and 30. I finished with a solid 15, but my overall performance was not good. We learned a lot about ourselves that game and that we had to become tougher to compete against that level of competition.

We won our next game and finished third place in our tournament. That was pretty much the tale of the rest of our season. We were very inconsistent. Don't get me wrong; we had a good team, but we struggled to bring it all together.

Our season ended and it was time for everybody to start making their college decisions. We were all disappointed on how our season went, but it was Coach Hutchins' first year as head coach and we played a really tough schedule. I was not use to losing, so it was tough on me. New Hampton was known for its great tradition in basketball and the team that year could have broken the tradition. There were a lot of things that I felt I could have done differently that season, but it was over and we couldn't get the season back so it was time to move on.

The goal Tori and I had set for ourselves was seeming more reachable every day. Mississippi State University coaches were flying up to watch me work out and the University of South Carolina's football coaches were in contact with Tori. Mississippi State offered me a visit and I took it shortly after. It was the third visit that I had been on since the season was over, the first two being Louisiana Monroe and Bradley University.

My mom and my uncle drove from Kentucky to Starkville, Mississippi to meet me. The visit went pretty well. I enjoyed the warm weather and hanging out with their players, but I told my mom, "There is no way I could go to this school. Look how country it is." At first she agreed. There were no malls and from what I saw there was only one main street. I grew up in a city and was ready to be back in that type of setting, especially after my year at the secluded New Hampton School. However, my mom pointed out that a small town with not much to get into could be a good thing. It would be easier to focus on basketball and schoolwork.

Before I went to bed Saturday night, my mom and I decided that even though we had enjoyed our visit, we were not ready to commit and thought we should go home and talk it over. The next morning my mom, uncle, and I had breakfast with the coaching staff before I had to leave for the airport. The head coach, Rick Stansbury, started putting the heat on me. Coach Stansbury asked me if I had enjoyed my visit. I smiled and nodded my head. His demeanor was intense. I knew what he was about to ask. The room was silent and everyone had tuned into our conversation. I was rubbing my hands together and tapping my feet. I was trying my best to stay calm. Coach grabbed my hand and said, "When are you going to make your decision?" I paused for a few seconds, looked at my mom and looked back at Coach Stansbury. I thought I had rehearsed the response to this question with my mom the night before, but I looked up at Coach Stansbury and said, "I'm coming." The room lit up with joy. The coaching staff all jumped out of their seats and started clapping and congratulating each other and me. I thought, "Wow, what did I just do?" I was worried my mom would be upset, but she had a big smile on her face. Even though she had told me not to commit, I knew this had to be a relief for her. After everything we had been through, her son was going to college to get an education. The situation was difficult for me because I hate being put on the spot, but it was time to grow up and I felt like I made the decision on my own. This decision wasn't anyone else's to make. I was a Mississippi State Bulldog.

Once I was through security at the airport I called Tori to tell him the good news. He was excited for me and told me some great news as well. Earlier that morning he had committed to South Carolina. I was so happy for both of us and I began tearing up on the phone. Both of us were yelling to each other, "We did it!" We accomplished our goal. We both signed with an SEC school.

The news spread quickly. My decision to commit to Mississippi State was all over the scouting websites. A lot of my friends were calling to congratulate me. The response I received from people was much more positive than the response I had received when I committed to IUPUI. Of course, I still had some doubters and people that felt like I shouldn't have committed there, but I wasn't letting anybody ruin this day for me. I got on that plane, closed my eyes, and just thought, "Wow, who would have ever thought I would be living this life?" I wasn't going to wear Kentucky across my chest, but I was going to have the opportunity to play against my dream school and show them what they missed out on. Let's go, Bulldogs!

***

Chapter 8:

WELCOME TO MISSISSIPPI

I looked over at Pops and asked, "Are we there yet?" I was just waking up from a long nap.

Pops said, "No, Twany, we still have about three more hours left." We had only been driving for about five hours, but it felt like it had been longer than that. I looked out the windows and all I could see was flat land, dirt roads, and cows close to the road. It was one of the scariest drives I've ever been on. There were maybe two houses every mile and I couldn't even remember seeing a gas station. The car was crammed with all of my belongings, mostly tennis shoes. I expressed to Pops several times how nervous I was during this drive. He thought it was funny. The cows were so close to the road, any wrong turn and we could have bumped into one of them. "This is Mississippi for you, Twany," Pops said jokingly.

I was already experiencing life of the country side.

Two more hours went past and suddenly we arrived on the big, beautiful campus of Mississippi State. The school popped out of nowhere. I was happy to be on campus and was ready to adjust to college life. It was early June when I arrived on campus and it was hot as could be. I was the first player to arrive on campus for summer school. Pops drove me to school a few days early because he was worried I wouldn't fix my room correctly, get my books, and learn my way around campus without someone helping me. I had to remind Pops that I wasn't a little kid anymore, but he didn't care. I'm happy Pops took me to school early for those reasons because he made sure that I took care of my responsibilities.

Summer school started off on a good note. Classes and summer conditioning were going well. There was hardly anyone on campus besides the athletic teams, so Starkville was kind of dead. If I were not in class or working out with the team, I was in my room listening to music or watching movies.

Coach brought in three freshmen that year: Dee Bost, Romero Osby, and me. Dee and Romero had a prior relationship before coming to Mississippi State, so they decided to be roommates and I was able to have my own room. I would have liked a roommate, but I also love having my own space. Dee and I were recruited to play the same position and you could feel the tension between us from day one. I didn't know anything about Dee signing with Mississippi State and he claimed he had no clue about the school signing me. On my visit, it was never mentioned and it was probably bad on my part because I didn't do enough research on whom they were recruiting. From conditioning drills, to weightlifting, to even pickup games at night, Dee and I competed against each other in everything. The team embraced the competition between us. They always encouraged it. It got to the point where Dee and I wouldn't even speak to each other. Some teammates were taking his side and some were taking mine. It was a weird situation. I didn't want to be going through anything like that my first year of college. I wanted to be friends and cool with everybody, but that was the situation and I had to fight my way through it. It wasn't anything new to me. I've had to fight and compete for everything my whole life. Dee was a really good point guard. I knew I had my hands full. He was about 6'2'', lightening quick, could shoot the 3, and could pass really well. He didn't have many weaknesses. My advantages were that I was 6'5'', stronger, and I felt like I was a more natural point guard than he was.

The tension got a little more intense when the coaches told me I couldn't wear number 3 because it was already assigned to Dee. On my visit, the coaches had promised me that I would be wearing number 3. I wore number 3 in high school and it was my favorite number. I was pissed. I wanted to leave the school when this situation arose. It took Pops to calm me down. He suggested for me to use it as motivation and went on and on about how the number on the back of the jersey didn't mean anything. It was another hurdle I was going to have to get over. My teammates heard about the jersey situation and turned it into a joke, but I didn't let it affect me.

The hostility spilled over into the first day of official practice. In the first drill, Dee and I were matched up against each other. We got tangled up and the emotions let loose. He said something to me that I didn't like and I pushed him and also shared a little of my mind. We were in each other's faces going back and forth until the coaches and our teammates got in between us. It actually got me excited. I was ready to compete and so was he. Every practice was pretty much that way. Dee and I went at it every day. It was good for both of us. We were making each other better.

During a practice about a week before our first exhibition game, I got a steal and broke out for a layup. When I came down, I landed on Dee's foot and fractured my foot. This injury sidelined me for almost four weeks and I lost the battle to Dee. Shortly after, he was named the starting point guard for the season. I rehabbed as much as possible and did what I could do to get back healthy. We started the season and Dee was off to a great start. At first, I was selfish and had hoped he wouldn't play well, but at the end of the day he was my teammate and I wanted to see us win.

A couple of games went past and we found ourselves on the road for our first away game. We were playing St. Bonaventure, which was a nice road test. It was a sold-out arena, and their crowd was as loud as I had ever heard a crowd before. I was cleared to play, but I didn't expect to play much

58

because I was fresh off an injury. Dee got in early foul trouble and had a couple of uncharacteristic turnovers. I heard "TWANY" come from down by the coaches and I looked at the coaches like "me?" I immediately started smiling and made my way to the check in table. You could tell my teammates were anxious to see how I would play during my first game. When I checked into the game we were losing, their crowd was going crazy, and St. Bonaventure had all of the momentum. I had not mentally prepared myself to be thrown into the fire so soon. I was rattled. The buzzer sounded and I checked in for Dee. My teammates on the court even looked surprised that I was thrown into that situation. I took a deep breath, closed my eyes, and said to myself, "Forget everything else; let's ball."

Immediately I had an impact. I scored four quick points and threw a couple of nice passes for buckets. We had the momentum now. I remember looking up at the clock and realizing I was getting a lot of minutes. The point guard for St. Bonaventure was 5'7'' and I was making it tough on him with my length and my ability to play strong defense. In that little span, coach gained a lot of confidence in me and left me in the game. It was a two-point game with about 40 seconds left on the clock. I had the ball dribbling up top. I slashed in the lane and made a pass to one of my teammates for a three. That three put us up five and gave us the BALLGAME. All my coaches and teammates congratulated me, except Dee. I was so hyped after the game.

I figured I would now have an opportunity to at least

split minutes with Dee, but that was not the case. Our very next game, we played Texas Tech in New Jersey and I only played about three minutes. I'm not sure why. Coach didn't give me a chance that game. Coming off the game against St. Bonaventure, I thought that I would at least get a chance. That was pretty much the tale for the rest of the season. I played sparingly, but I played pretty well in the minutes that I received.

It was late February and time for my homecoming. The University of Kentucky was up next on the schedule. I was excited about playing against my dream school. It was also going to be the first time I was going to play a college game in front of my mom and most of my family. With travel and Mom's schedule it was hard for her to make it down to Starkville, Mississippi.

Running out onto the court at Rupp brought back so many memories. My emotions were running high. Kentucky that year was struggling. I knew that if we played well we would have a chance to win in Rupp, which does not happen often. I warned my teammates about how big Rupp was and how loud the fans were. They did a pretty good job of adjusting. Our coaches put together a great game plan and it worked almost perfectly. We trapped Patrick Patterson and tried to force someone else to beat us. UK struggled shooting from the outside that night and we made almost everything. I got in, made my first shot, and was super hyped. My homecoming was going pretty well. We ended up winning the game and it felt like we had beat the number one team in the nation. Winning that game meant a lot to me, but it also meant a lot to our head coach, one of our assistants, and one of my other teammates who were also from the state of Kentucky. We all wanted that win very badly. I didn't play as many minutes as I would have liked, but I was just happy that we got the win.

We finished the regular season with a record of 18-12 and were not considered an NCAA tournament team, but we got hot at the right time and won four straight games. We were crowned SEC Tournament champions. That was one of the happiest moments of my life. We were champions and no one thought we could do it. We were on the court celebrating with cameras and graffiti all around us. I remember someone handing me an SEC sign and I held it up to the crowd. My Pops, who was sitting right behind the bench, was yelling at me to flip the sign. Once I understood what he was telling me, I looked up at the sign and realized it was upside down. Instead of the crowd seeing SEC, the crowd was seeing an upside down CES. By the time I corrected the sign it was almost too late. Pictures were already out online and my friends were calling me laughing about it. It was so embarrassing, but still didn't take away from the moment. Later on that next week, we went on to lose in the first round of the NCAA tournament to Washington.

Going into my sophomore year at Mississippi State, we had high hopes. The leading shot blocker in the country, Jarvis Varnado, and sharp shooter Barry Stewart, were returning for their senior years as well as several key players from the previous year. Dee and I still competed against each other at a high level, but the hostility between us had faded and we were becoming friends. The coaches were even mentioning Dee and me playing on the court at the same time a lot that year.

Once again, an obstacle was thrown my way. This time it was a big one. My hips started hurting one day and I had no clue what it was or why. I was trying to fight through it. It felt like someone was stabbing me in the hips every time I bent down to play defense. I tried to go without telling anybody and tried my best to fight through it. I couldn't show any signs of weakness. I was taking medicine before practice every day just to get me through, but when that stopped working I knew it had to be something serious. At that point, I went to the trainer and told him what I was going through. The trainer scheduled an MRI immediately.

It took two long days of nervous waiting for the MRI results to come back. The MRI results showed that my hips were in bad shape and I was sent to Nashville to meet with hip specialist Dr. J.W. Thomas Byrd. I kept this on the hush from my teammates as much as I could because I didn't want a bunch of people to know what was going on. Dr. Byrd told me the worst news I had ever heard in my life. He informed me that I had bone spurs on both of my hips and both labrums were torn. He said he had no clue how I had been playing basketball in the condition my hips were in. He told me that surgery was needed as soon as possible which would put me out a whole year.

I cried like a baby right in front of Dr. Byrd. Pops was in the room with me and broke down as well. I had never seen Pops cry; his emotion made me realize how much he had grown to care for me. I thought my career was over. I felt like I couldn't catch a break in life. I was asking myself, "Why me? Why does this always have to happen to me?" Dr. Byrd told me to calm down and that everything would be alright. I was thinking about what my coaches would think and how they would react and what my mom would think and how she would react. I was really emotional. If there was any point in my life when I felt like giving up and throwing in the towel, it was then. I was on the verge of having my break out season at a Division I college and in the blink of an eye, that moment I had been waiting for my whole life was taken away from me. I couldn't wrap my mind around why this was happening. The news from Dr. Byrd broke me all the way down. For the first time in my life I realized that the life I had always envisioned for myself might not be the life that I was going to live. I felt lost and confused. What was my plan in life? What was God trying to tell me?

Once the news reached my teammates and coaches, they were all sad about losing me for the season. During those times, it felt good to see people show me that they cared about me. My mom was scared to death about me having surgery. She was hesitant and worried something would go wrong.

That year I had two successful surgeries with Dr. Byrd and rehabbed to the best of my ability. My hips were in way better shape than they were before surgery. After 10 months, I was ready to start training again. Not being able to play basketball for 10 months made this the longest 10 months of my life. You don't realize how much something means to you until it gets taken away from you. I had never gone that long without touching a basketball since I was a little kid. A part of me was missing. I needed distractions to keep my mind off of not being able to play basketball. I enjoyed having my friends around who were full of jokes that kept me laughing.

My team finished the season 23-12. That year Jarvis Varnado broke the all-time shot blocking record in the history of college basketball and Barry Stewart broke the record for most three pointers made in the history of Mississippi State. Like my freshman year, the team got hot during the SEC tournament and went on to face a very tough Kentucky team in the championship. That Kentucky team included John Wall, DeMarcus Cousins, Eric Bledsoe, and Patrick Patterson, just to name a few. A rebound put back by DeMarcus Cousins with .2 seconds left on the clock forced the game into overtime. Kentucky outplayed us in overtime and went on to win the SEC Championship. Losing that game really hurt because our NCAA tournament hopes were on the line and we needed that game. To lose it the way we did was devastating. We ended up not making the NCAA tournament and lost in the second round of the NIT to North Carolina.

Sights were set on my junior year. By redshirting I now was a junior in the classroom, but just a sophomore on the court. My hips were fixed and my body was in great shape. After last season ended Dee entered the NBA draft, but failed to appropriately withdraw his name before the deadline. By doing so, Dee was suspended for the first semester of the season. That left me to be the only point guard on the roster, and this was the perfect opportunity for me to step up.

The season started off very slow and we lost some games we shouldn't have lost. Our head coach was all over me about every little thing. It took me a little time to get used to playing again because I had been out so long. I played well in some games, but not so well in others. I was starting, but there was some part of me that was not enjoying it. The team that year was not as close as the previous two teams. There was a lot of animosity among each other and things were just different. Gradually frustration started to build and I just wasn't happy. Finally, after two years, I got to be the starting point guard and I still wasn't satisfied. I tried to understand why I felt like this, but there wasn't really a clear reason. I mentioned transferring and relocating to another school to my mom and that idea did not sit very well with her. I also ran the same scenario across to Pops, and he felt the same way my mom did. Neither one of them thought I should try to transfer because I was so close to graduating. I then figured that I would suck it up and try to make myself happy, but that was easier said than done. Over Christmas break Mississippi State played in a tournament held in Hawaii. The team was sitting together watching a game and two of my teammates were involved in an altercation with each other in the stands. Mississippi State received a lot of bad publicity after this incident. This was the last straw for me. Transferring seemed like my only option. When we got back to school after the tournament I sat down with the coaches and expressed my unhappiness. They were all kind of surprised. I usually hide the way I feel so I could see how they were blinded by it. The coaches and I all came to an agreement that I was making the right decision. I made sure that I was leaving the program on great terms with no hard feelings from either side. It was tough to leave the teammates that I had played with for three years and also the friends that I had met in the Starkville community. I was really emotional leaving the coaches' office because I didn't know where my life was headed. I felt bad to break ties with the school and coaching staff who gave me the opportunity to attend college and play basketball, but I felt like I was making the best decision for me. My decision was bold because I had not contacted any other schools. I was not sure where I would end up, but I knew that sometimes people have to risk everything to gain something better.

Halfway back to Louisville I reached over in the passenger's seat and grabbed my release form. As I was reading it, I noticed that Mississippi State had not prohibited me from transferring to another SEC school. Usually when a player transfers, the former institution will not allow a player to transfer to another school in the same conference. So I immediately started thinking…

***

Chapter 9:
BACK IN THE BLUEGRASS

Here I was in my first practice for the University of Kentucky and I found myself guarding Brandon Knight, who was the starting point guard. I was playing defense like I never had before. I was being physical and making it hard for Brandon to initiate the offense. I had a lot of energy and was very enthusiastic. I was trying to prove myself. I quickly caught the eye of the coaches. Coach Cal and his assistants applauded me several times during that practice about the defense I was playing on Brandon. Players were also taking notice of how hard I was playing. This practice was in mid-season, which is around the time where practices are lighter on contact and not as intense. The players seemed to be wondering why I was playing so hard. I don't think they realized that I was fighting for my life and trying to prove to the coaches that I belonged. I was now living my dream. All these years I had dreamed about playing for the University of Kentucky and now it was a reality.

That day taught me a lot about myself as a basketball player. I got the sense that defense would be my niche while playing for Coach Cal. That day also let me know that I could play and compete with some of the best players in the country. The team that year had three McDonald All-American players in Terrence Jones, Doron Lamb, and Brandon Knight. The team also had a few solid experienced players in Darius Miller, Josh Harrellson and DeAndre Liggins. Up to this point in my life that was the most talented team I had ever been a part of and I was ready for the challenge. I could not play in games due to the NCAA transferring rules, so I made it a point to give it everything I had in practice. I tried to compete hard every day to make my teammates better. I was a 6'5'' point guard who could handle the ball, pass it really well, and play ball-hawking defense. I gave the team another solid Division I player to compete against every day.

After a couple days of practice, I was called to the officeto meet with Coach Cal. This was scary because I didn't knowwhat it was about or what he was going to say to me. I immediately began to think negatively. I began thinking that he may tell me I'm not good enough and I should pack my bags and head home. Then I thought about how well I had been practicing and started realizing the meeting may not be that bad. It was one of those times that I just didn't know what to expect and I had to be ready for whatever came my way. I strolled into Coach Cal's office with a big smile on my face, hiding all of my fear of what I was expecting. "What's up, Coach? How are you doing?" I said as calmly as I could.

Coach said, "Call your mom and tell her we will be putting you on scholarship."

I replied, "Do what, Coach?" As he repeated what he had said to me, I wanted to just grab him and hug him as tight as I could and just thank him. Initially, Coach Cal offered me a walk on spot and that meant that I would have had to pay my way through school and also pay for food and lodging. This was a big help for my family because my mom could not afford to pay for my schooling since I had two younger brothers at home that needed all of her assistance. When I called my mom and told her the news, she was as happy as could be. Mom initially wasn't a fan of me leaving Mississippi State, but with me reaching my dream school she began to accept my decision.

Life for me changed quickly. I no longer was just Twany Beckham, I was now Twany Beckham who plays for the University of Kentucky. Everywhere I went people noticed me and would come up and speak and ask for pictures and sometimes autographs. Students on campus would congratulate me and welcome me to the team as they would walk past me. I remember Coach Cal sending out a tweet asking the Big Blue Nation to welcome me to the team and my twitter followers jumped a couple thousand within 24 hours. I knew then that this was going to be something special and my life was headed in the right direction. It was the attention that I'd always wanted, so I was embracing it and was thankful every day that I was getting that opportunity.

With all of the positive attention, I knew there had to be some negative attention involved as well. There were people who thought I made a poor decision by going to Kentucky. I heard things like "you will never play" and "you're not a McDonald All-American. Coach Cal doesn't care about you." I laughed at all the negative criticism. It was funny to me. How could someone know what my future would be like? Even if those people were right, I still wanted to challenge myself and hope for the best.

I felt like some of my friends and family began to view me differently. People that I had not heard from in a while were all of sudden calling me and wanting to associate themselves with me. I was getting ticket requests for games. Since I was from Louisville, people were especially trying to lock in tickets for the Louisville game next season. I thought, "Wow, this is going to be crazy when I become eligible to play."

We were wrapping up regular season play and were struggling to win close games on the road. Out of eight conference road games that year, we fell short in six of them. A road game for Kentucky is not the same for any other program in the country. During a road game it's like the Kentucky coaches and players versus the other team, their city, and the refs. Whatever team Kentucky plays it is like their Super Bowl. A school can have average to below average attendance at games, but when Kentucky comes to town, it's a sellout. It has been like that for years and I don't think that it is ever going to change. As good of players as Kentucky always has, winning road games will always be a tough task. It helps playing for Coach Cal who embraces the challenges of playing on the road. Coach has always had good teams who were targets when playing away from home, so he knows how to coach in those situations. The confidence that Coach Cal instills in his teams gives them the ability to prosper in any situation.

Due to NCAA regulations, I could not travel on the road with the team, but watched every game very closely. Losing six road games in conference play might have seemed like a lot, but what Coach Cal was impressed about was the fight that the team showed. The fight in our team showed during the SEC Tournament. The team won three games in a row and was crowned SEC Tourney Champs. I was happy for my teammates and the success they were having, but I wanted to be a part of it. I was practicing every day, but couldn't reap the benefits.

The first couple of rounds of the NCAA tournament went by like a blur. A couple of tight games and a few clutch game-winning shots by Brandon Knight and our team found itself going to Houston to compete in the Final Four. My team was going to compete in the Final Four and I couldn't go. This was so devastating to me. Going to a Final Four is a once-in-a-lifetime opportunity for some people, so who knew if I would ever get that opportunity again? As the team was loading up the bus heading for the airport, a bunch of fans were standing outside cheering and wishing the team good luck. I stood in front of the bus and hugged every player and wished them good luck. They could all see in my eyes that I wanted to go to the Final Four with them, but I was not allowed. Some of my teammates lightly rubbed it in by saying things like "Twany, wish you could go with us" or "Twany, you're going to miss one hell of a trip."

I got emotional because I had that feeling that we could win the national championship and I wouldn't be able to celebrate with my team. As the bus pulled off, I watched the bus for about two blocks before it turned onto another street. I thought, "What am I going to do for these next couple of days?" I was the only one that would be staying in the lodge. There would be no practice in the afternoons, so I had all the time to relax and focus on getting my school work done.

Every day ESPN would showcase behind-the-scenes coverage of my team participating in Final Four activities such as media, photo shoots, and commercial recordings. It looked like they were having such a ball. I would call some of my teammates just to see how things were going and they would all say the same thing, "Houston is live. We wish you were here with us." The message I always told them was to remain focused and to keep their eyes on the prize.

Growing up in Kentucky I knew how big this was to be in the Final Four and have a chance at winning the national championship for the University of Kentucky. There was no time for the guys to not be focused. Anticipation for the games was probably the worst thing that I went through. Days leading up to the game seemed so long and drawn out. I got tired of hearing college basketball analysts state their predictions about who would win. I was ready for some basketball to be played and to watch my brothers compete on the big stage.

The day had come and it was time for my team to go out and play some ball. Downtown Lexington was full of UK fans packing into bars and restaurants preparing for the game. A bunch of my friends came to Lexington to take in the day with me. We walked around downtown Lexington and had a blast. All the fans were high fiving me and reminding me that next year was my year to experience all of this. My friends who were from Louisville were blown away by how the fans were acting. They were wishing they had played for UK. It was nothing but positivity and love from every fan. The main reason I went out there to walk around was to show some appreciation. It was kind of crazy to me that every fan out there knew exactly who I was. They were just so nice to me. How could you not love the Big Blue Nation?

Game time was approaching. My friends and I went back to a friend's house and all gathered around the television in the common area. The game was over before we knew it and my brothers had come up short to Connecticut in the national semifinal game. I could not have been prouder of my brothers by the way they fought and played their hearts out. On that night, Connecticut was the better team and they went on to win the national championship. We were so close to bringing number eight back to the city of Lexington, but with the return of Terrence Jones, Doron Lamb, Darius Miller, and the number one recruiting class coming in we knew we would make another run at it.

***

Chapter 10:
ONE HEARTBEAT

The month of May was winding down and it was almost time for everyone to report to campus for summer school. We had the number one recruiting class coming in. That class consisted of Anthony Davis, Michael Kidd-Gilchrist, Marquis Teague, and Kyle Wiltjer to go along with our returning players. When I sat back and looked at the scenario I could have easily said that there would be no playing time for me on this team, but I refused to think like that. I've always felt like I was just as good as the next person regardless of any rankings and that if I worked harder than the next person my opportunity would come. I had spent the whole month of May training and getting in shape. I wanted to be ready to compete from day one. I conditioned, worked on my shooting, and tightened up my ball handling skills. Due to transferring I would not be eligible to play until mid-December, so I already had that going against me. What I had to focus on was being ready when I became eligible for any opportunity that could present itself and taking full advantage of it.

It was June 1st and everyone on the team was arriving on campus for summer school. This team had special written all over it. From day one our bond as a team was as tight as it could get, granted all of the recruits had previously known each other from playing AAU basketball games against each other and also playing in a few previous all-star games. It shocked me how quickly that we all came together and formed that bond. Most of the team took the same classes so we would all walk to class together, eat lunch together, and head to workouts together. About two or three times a week we would do team activities like go to the movies, batting cages, putt putt golf, and bowling. At nights, several teammates would get together and go in the gym to work out.

From day one the topic of our conversation was always winning the national championship. We created the phrase "national championship or failure" and that became our team motto for the rest of the season. I knew once I saw guys in the gym at night always working and the way we went hard as a team during workouts, individuals, and conditioning that it was going to be a special year. Workouts were so competitive. Guys would fight their hardest just to win drills and pickup games during the week. In pickup games, we would set teams and the team that you were on played together for the entire week. At the end of each week, we would keep a score of how many games each team won and go to the coaching staff and brag about it. The games were so competitive, nobody wanted to lose. If you lost you knew that the other team would go bragging to the coaching staff and you didn't want to be on the team that Coach Cal always heard was losing. It was a pride thing.

For those freshmen to come in and be as competitive as they were spoke volumes for what kind of players they were. I rely on my competitiveness to get me through in basketball, but from playing against guys like Michael Kidd-Gilchrist, Marquis Teague, and Anthony Davis every day my competitiveness went up another level. You had to practically get into a fist fight if you were caught up in any physical contact on the basketball court with Kidd-Gilchrist and Teague. Coach Cal was happy with the progress that everyone was making and I was excited about our team.

Over the summer I developed a close relationship with Anthony Davis. Anthony was like a little brother to me. From day one, he and I had this connection almost like the one that I had with my prep school roommate Tori Gurly. Anthony never went out and I didn't either, so we both would sit in the dorm all hours of the night and just talk about life. I learned a lot about him, where he came from, and how he grew up and I told him a lot about me, and where I came from, and how I grew up. Most of the time we would talk about what we thought the season would be like and I would always try to give him advice on how physical teams would play him because he was so skinny. Just like me, Anthony had that "I don't fear anyone" attitude and I think that's what drew me closer to him.

We would talk about what we thought the NBA life would be like and how we would change the lives of our families. Some nights got more emotional than others. One thing that I always told Anthony was that no matter how much fame he got to always remain humble and never forget where he came from. With Anthony being this big-time recruit and one of the best players in the country, I sometimes wondered why he would listen to me and the advice that I would give him. With me being a junior in college, I was one of the oldest on the team and just tried to be a leader to all of my teammates. There would be nights I would be sound asleep with an 8:00 a.m. class and Anthony would come in my room at 3:00 a.m. trying to talk.

Darius Miller and I had a close relationship as well. I had known Darius since the 6th grade and over the years, we managed to maintain a good relationship. When I first joined the UK basketball team, Darius was the person who took me under his wing and showed me the ropes. Since Darius was one of the older players on the team I tried to learn a lot from him.

At the end of July, everyone got to go home for about two weeks before fall semester began. No one on the team wanted to leave. We all wanted to stay in Lexington with each other. Summer school had gone by too fast. When I was home visiting with my family, all I could think about was my team and how much fun we had that summer. We all kept in touch with each other during those two weeks and everyone was anxious to get back to school. Everywhere I went while I was home in Louisville, I told everyone that this year Kentucky would win a national championship and most people agreed. However, some people, especially Louisville fans, didn't take that comment too well. All I would say was "We will see." I would brag about how good our team was going to be to everybody back at home that I knew were Louisville fans. I told them that Louisville had no shot of beating us in Rupp Arena that year.

I arrived back on campus two days before classes started, but most of my teammates were not expected to be back until the next day. I wanted to get there a day early to make sure I had everything organized so I wasn't up late trying to do things the night before classes. I also wanted to get in the gym before anyone else did to get some conditioning in and to put up a few shots. That's just how I was. I always felt like I needed to be more prepared than the next person. This year I definitely felt the need to be more prepared because I was on such a talented team.

When I woke up the next morning, I went over to the Joe Craft Center and Kidd-Gilchrist and a few other players were already in the gym. These guys could not have been back for more than an hour or two and they were already in the gym working out. That alone inspired me. These guys were freshmen and acting like veterans. You just don't expect freshmen to come into college with that kind of work ethic and mindset. It usually takes freshmen a year to adjust. I was in my fourth year of college and just starting to understand the true meaning of hard work. I've always been a hard worker, but these guys were some of the best high school players in the country and were not settling on that.

I hopped in the workouts with the guys. After putting up a lot of shots, Anthony, Kidd-Gilchrist, Teague and I decided to play cut throat. Cut throat is a game where as a team we would pick a score that has to be reached. Two people play one-on-one and the person who reaches the set score first wins. If the offensive person scores the ball, he gets to stay on offense and the next person in line steps on for defense. I was playing pretty well and making a lot of tough shots. I was trying to gain the respect of my teammates. Whenever I was on defense, I made it a point to not let my man score. I made it hard on whoever had the ball with my physical defense.

The game was almost unfair when Anthony was on defense. His shot blocking ability made it so hard for anyone to get off a shot. I had never seen anything like it. One time he was standing at the free throw line and I jumped up to take a three-point shot and he blocked the ball in my face. I immediately started laughing. I was like "no way did that just happen." I watched Teague and Kidd-Gilchrist consistently drive around Anthony and think they had easy layups, but Anthony would pin their balls on the glass. We were playing our hearts out. No one wanted to lose. I ended up winning a game or two, but Kidd-Gilchrist and Anthony won the majority. After we had played, Kidd-Gilchrist said, "Twan, I didn't know you was that tough." Teague and Anthony basically said the same thing. They gave me some confidence about myself and I had hoped that I could play that way all the time. The next day coaches had heard about the cut throat games and were all happy that we were in the gym putting in some extra work and getting to know one another as teammates. Coach Cal was all about team bonding. He preached over and over to us about hanging out together and doing team-oriented activities. Coach Cal has been in this business for a very long time so we all knew that he knew what he was talking about.

The first couple weeks of fall semester went pretty well. All the players had classes in the morning, so all of our afternoons would be free for workouts and conditioning. We would condition and lift weights three times a week and play pickup games on the other days. Coach Cal, who was on the road a lot during the early fall semester, would call in to the strength coaches to check on our progress. Sometimes Coach Cal would have the team meet in his office and he would talk to us through speaker phone. Every team meeting always ended with Coach Cal telling us that he could not wait to get back to Lexington. We would all be excited about hearing from our coach since we did not see him that much during those times.

Around this time, the NBA lockout situation was going on and guys like myself and a few others on the team got some once-in-a-lifetime experiences. With the NBA locked out, some of their players were looking for places to play pickup ball and luckily, Lexington, Kentucky, was the destination. Several former UK players came, such as Tayshaun Prince, Eric Bledsoe, DeMarcus Cousins, Josh Harrellson, and DeAndre Liggins. Rajon Rondo invited some of his Boston Celtics teammates and Nazr Mohammed invited some of his Oklahoma City teammates, such as Kevin Durant and Russell Westbrook. Even LeBron James was in attendance. There were enough players to have pickup games going on in the Joe Craft Center's men's and women's gyms.

Everyone on our team was hyped because this was an opportunity to play against NBA players and measure up our individual skills against professionals. We were playing against some of the best players in the world. I grew up playing against Rondo so I wasn't nervous at all to play against him, but for the few plays I was matched up with LeBron in the post I may have been as nervous as I have ever been. I was guarding someone else when a shot went up and LeBron got the rebound. No one on my team was guarding him and I was the closest man so I just took him. So many things ran through my head, but the first thought was to not get dunked on. I was hoping he shot a fade away jump shot or something to let me off the hook. Instead he made a spin move so quick that it left me in my tracks. By the time I turned around I could just see the back of LeBron as he was going up for a two-handed dunk.

I don't know how in the world he made that spin move that quick. I wanted to put up more fight than that, but, hey, he is the best player in the world.

I remember guarding Kevin Durant one time. He posted me and made a shot that no human being on a regular day would attempt to take. On another possession, Durant came down the court dribbling the ball through his legs. I was low and ready to play some physical defense. He turned his back and shot a fade away three a few feet behind the three-point line and drained it. All net. I just put my hand up in the air and looked around. Terrence Jones who was on my team looked at me and said, "It's Kevin Durant, bro; don't be ashamed."

Overall, I had a good week of games against the professional players. Most of my teammates stood out, some more than others. The way that Anthony and Terrence played, you would have thought that they were already professional players. I'm not a fan of the NBA locking out its players, but I was grateful for the opportunity it gave our team. I think playing well against those professionals for a week straight gave our team the confidence that we could play well against any college team in the country.

I learned a lot that week not just from playing basketball, but from observing and interacting with the professional players. I would ask questions about the NBA lifestyle and how much fun it was to be an NBA player. My main question was what it was like to have all of that money.

After talking to these guys, the main thing they would say was enjoy college because you can never get it back. I overheard LeBron telling someone that he wished he had gone to college. From talking with former Wildcat Nazr Mohammed, I got a glimpse of how hard professional athletes actually worked. He told me that while the professional players had been in Lexington, they all worked out three times a day. They would get up in the morning to lift weights. In the afternoons they would do on court workouts and conditioning. At night they would play pickup with us. Nazr made the statement to me that basketball is like a full-time job. You have to love it to be able to maintain. Until this conversation with Nazr, I had always thought that making it to the NBA meant that my dream had been reached and that was the end of the road. My thought process had been distracted with thoughts of money and the NBA lifestyle. I never really considered how hard work and dedication would have to be maintained or even increased in order to remain an NBA player.

Even as a collegiate player, basketball was like a full-time job. Combining the time you have to spend in your sport along with the time you have to spend on academics is very hard. A typical day for my teammates and I started with us waking up at 6 a.m. for weight lifting or conditioning. From 8 a.m. to 2 p.m. we had to make sure we got two meals in our systems and attend all of our classes. Practice every day was held between the times of 2:30 p.m. and 5:00 p.m. After practice, we had team dinner and tutoring sessions usually followed. If you had two or three tutoring sessions you could be in the academic center until about 10:00 at night. Coach Cal was big on guys getting in the gym at night to work on their game, so after tutoring sessions guys normally went to the gym. After night workouts were over we usually got back to our dorms about 11:30 p.m. or 12:00 a.m. A normal day for us was so demanding that it was hard to find time for other activities. I put a lot of energy into my studies, so there were many nights I found myself up until the wee hours of the morning studying.

During the times when we got the opportunity to go out in public, whether it was doing community service, working Coach Cal's camps, or even taking team trips to the mall, people got a chance to socialize with us and were always surprised by how nice and friendly we were. Most people think of athletes as being arrogant and cocky, when in all actuality that is very misleading. My teammates and I had this same misconception. People didn't know how friendly and nice we were until they got the opportunity to meet us. On an average school day most of us would walk to class with our headphones in and barely socialize, but it wasn't due to the case of being arrogant or cocky. More than likely morning workouts had drained us and we were just trying to get to class as quickly as possible. During my entire five years in college, I don't think I ear went to class without my headphones. There were times I was late to class trying to find my headphones in my room.

Signing autographs and taking pictures with people is something that I grew to enjoy while at the University of Kentucky. At first, I used to always down play the fact that people would want my autograph and want to take pictures with me. It was something that took a little while to get used to. I realized that UK fans loved you no matter what contributions you gave to the team. If you were on the roster, you were someone special to the Big Blue Nation. From the first day I joined the team, the fans showed me a lot of love and treated me the same way they treated those that were playing all the minutes.

It was a week before Big Blue Madness and I was getting really nervous. It was going to be my first ever Big Blue Madness and it was also going to be my first time playing in front of UK fans. Big Blue Madness is one of the greatest traditions in all of college basketball. On the first official day of college basketball practice, UK fans pack Rupp Arena to welcome that year's men's and women's basketball teams. Every year there is something special about Big Blue Madness, whether it's the entertaining introductions or guest appearances. I had been to two previous Big Blue Madness events growing up as a fan. Rajon Rondo, who is a close friend of mine, participated in Big Blue Madness two times and I attended both to support him. When I was there in Rupp Arena supporting Rondo, I imagined what it would be like if I were out there participating. A few years later, there I was about to participate in my first Big Blue Madness as a player.

I loved the atmosphere on campus the entire week leading up to Big Blue Madness. Fans from all over came to UK's campus to camp out in tents to save a spot in line for tickets. I really liked how the University of Kentucky used Big Blue Madness as an opportunity for those fans who normally can't make it to home games to have first dibs at tickets by camping out. So many tents occupy UK's campus during this week that campus during this time of year has earned the name "Tent City." A few of the nights that week were extremely cold and I do not understand how people slept outside in tents. Each morning the coaching staff would order McDonald's breakfast and have the team deliver the meals throughout Tent City. It was actually a fun thing to do. I can remember going around yelling, "Wake up! Hot breakfast!" One time I opened up a tent to serve breakfast and there was a dad with four little kids all snuggled up, probably trying to use each other's body heat to keep warm. My emotions took over immediately. I wondered why a man would have four little kids out there in the cold just for a practice game. Then it also made me appreciate the fact that a man would go through all that just to see our team practice. It was a very humbling moment.

Even though the week leading up to Big Blue Madness was fun, it was also somewhat stressful. It would be the first time that I was able to have tickets to give to friends and family. All the players were allowed to have fifteen tickets to distribute. Almost everybody in my family and a lot of my friends wanted to attend and expected to attend. It was so stressful choosing the fifteen people I wanted to invite. Like most of my problems my entire life, I put it in my mom's hands. Luckily, she did a good job of picking and choosing fairly. Some of my family members and my childhood friends attended. My brother Mark, who was incarcerated, was able to watch from inside the jail. My mom told me that when I got introduced that night she would probably cry because I had reached a life-long dream of mine.

The night of Big Blue Madness came fast. It was time for our team to show why we were ranked top five in the country according to the preseason polls. That day I can remember being nervous, almost as if we had a game to play that night. We had an entirely new team and it was almost everybody's first time playing in Rupp Arena, so I could see a lot of nervous tension in the guys. Waiting backstage for the introductions drove me crazy. The longer the wait, the more nervous I got. I peeped out behind the curtain a few times and saw a packed Rupp Arena with fans going crazy. There was not a single empty seat and the fans were as loud as could be. In attendance that night sitting courtside were former UK players Rajon Rondo, DeAndre Liggins, DeMarcus Cousins, John Wall, Nazr Mohammed, and Tayshaun Prince. The NBA lockout was in effect so the former players had an opportunity to attend Madness. I turned to some of the guys and said, "It's finally here, boys. It's time to show the world what we're about."

The next thing I knew, I heard the PA announcer say,

"From Louisville, Kentucky, Twwaaaannnyyy Beeckammm". I walked onto the stage and looked into the crowd thinking "WOW! This is what Kentucky Basketball is all about right here, Baby!" I told all my friends that I would dance, but I froze up. I was so caught up in the moment that I forgot to dance. My mom was sitting to the right of the stage along with my family and friends who were all yelling and screaming. I pointed to them to let them know that I saw them and continued on down the stage. I shook hands with the fans who were sitting next to the stage and joined my teammates who had been called before me in the middle of the court.

After the whole team was introduced, Coach Cal gave the Kentucky Effect speech which ignited the whole crowd. He talked about the program being built on a foundation of integrity, class and "the gold standard of college basketball." He also mentioned Kentucky being a "player's first program" where athletes will love to play basketball "not only because of banners, rings or trophies but because this is the place where players dreams become reality." The speech had me on the edge of my seat. I caught myself clapping and applauding along with the crowd after every strong statement from Coach Cal. I sat there and listened nervously. The palms of my hands were extremely sweaty. I had sweat running down my forehead and we hadn't even gotten on the court yet.

We were now ready to play some basketball. Warm up line was all what it was cracked up to be. Everyone was bringing out their best dunks and the crowd was getting hyped.

I even pulled off a dunk or two strictly from adrenaline. I got a couple of "oohs" and "ahhs" from the crowd. My time as a UK basketball player was finally here. I subbed into the game about mid-way through the first half. My nerves had vanished. It was time to go now, no time to be nervous. When I checked in I looked over at Rondo and he kind of nodded his head to me as if to say, "Let's go." My night could not have gone any better. I immediately impacted the game with a no-look pass to Terrence Jones for a dunk. I followed up with a rebound and a smooth drive to the lane for a layup. I guarded Marquis Teague, who was the point guard for the other team. Even though this was a fun scrimmage, I took it as an opportunity for me to prove myself to the coaches. I played solid defense on Teague and tried to make it tough for him to score. I pushed the ball down the court as fast as I could and made great passing and play calling decisions. I was just trying to control the tempo of the game. The highlight of my night was catching an alley oop pass from Ryan Harrow and finishing it with a two-hand dunk. I was so hyped. I was really happy with the way I had performed.

After the game was over I walked over to Rondo and he said to me, "Tonight was one of the best nights I've ever seen you play. If you just play like that and keep working on your game, you will get a chance."

I shook his hand and said, "Thank you, big bro. I will continue to work." We looked really good as a team and all the new players proved to the fans why they had been highly recruited. When I got back to the locker room and checked my phone I had a ton of missed calls and text messages and my twitter was blowing up. People were tweeting me things like "You're going to be a great addition to this team" and "Glad you transferred to UK." I even got a few tweets saying "You have John Wall speed with the ball." I'm pretty fast with the ball, but no way do I have John Wall speed. It felt good coming off the court and receiving all this positive feedback.

I thought because I had played well in Big Blue Madness I would gain the respect of the coaches; however, this did not seem to be the case. Instead, Coach Cal was all over me. It seemed like I could not do anything right. I began to realize that Coach Cal was being harder on me because later this season I would be eligible to play in games. He started coaching me as hard as he coached the other players that could potentially play in games. I became introduced to the real Coach Calipari. At first, I did not respond well to this more intense version of Coach Cal. I had heard him yell and scream in practices before, but his directing those yells and screams towards me was different. Everything he said to me I took personally. Sometimes when Coach Cal would yell at me I would act stubborn and purposefully tune him out the rest of practice. Other times I would keep replaying something he had said to me in my head and miss details, new drills or plays we were learning. I would step on the court to run the new drill or play and I would be so confused that I would mess up, which gave Coach Cal another opportunity to get on me. Coach Cal started saying that he thought I was listening to music in my head. He would say this out loud in front of the team and all my teammates would just laugh. Until I figured out how to brush it off and move on, this affected me a great deal. At first, I took it as Coach Cal was making fun of me but in reality, he was only testing my mental toughness. I fell into the trap. Instead of keeping my head up and moving on to the next thing, I pouted and did exactly the opposite of what Coach Cal wanted me to do.

I quickly felt the pressure of trying to be a point guard for Coach Calipari even as a backup. I tried to take the easy way out and move to the wing position. Moving positions helped me, but I couldn't hide. I still found ways to get yelled at. I knew I was mentally tougher than what I was showing. At night in the dorms I would go to several of my teammates' rooms and just ask them what they thought I could do to get Coach Cal off my back. I would tell my teammates that I thought Coach Cal didn't like me and they would look at me like I was crazy. They would tell me that I would not be on the team if he didn't like me. Anthony and Darius would tell me to just relax in practice and play how I usually play. They also told me to not listen to how criticism comes out of Coach Cal's mouth and to just take in what he is saying. My response to them was that it is easier said than done. I tried to do what Anthony and Darius suggested. Coach would yell at me in practice and I reminded myself to look at him, nod my head, put aside any frustration, and focus on the meaning of his words.

After a while I started playing better in practice and started responding to his coaching better. It just took some adjusting. I would call home and explain to my mom what I was going through. My mom would just say, "You better be happy he's yelling at you. By him yelling at you it shows you that he cares and is only trying to help you." Little did I know, Coach Cal was just teaching me how to be a man. I grew up a lot during the first couple weeks of practice. I was becoming more mentally tough and learning to fight through adversity. I knew from the start that this would not be easy and that whatever I went through I just had to stay the course and not give up.

***

Chapter 11:
DREAM SEASON

Ranked number two in the nation, with all the expectations in the world, we were ready to go. The season was finally here. All the talking and looking at preseason magazines could finally be put to rest. It was time for the popcorn to be popped, the fans to start cheering, the ball to be tipped, and Coach Cal to start yelling. I was more than ready to get this show on the road. Unfortunately, eligibility rules were sidelining me until second semester. I could not dress with the team or travel, and during home games I could not dress in uniform. While the team was on the road I had to stay behind and watch the games from the dorm. I did not mind it much this time around because I knew that second semester would come quick. The best thing for me to do was to support my teammates and be the biggest cheerleader I could be.

The aura around this team was different from any team I had ever been on. As a team, we had a bond that was seamless and impermeable. Not only did our personalities complement each other, we were all unified by a common goal - a national championship - and we were not going to let anything get in the way.

Coach Cal told us right before the season started to remove any negativity from our lives, even if that meant some of our closest friends and family. Coach wanted no distractions and wanted us to remain one big family. He also made sure that girls were not going to cause problems. Almost every week during team meetings he would say, "If a girl says yes it means no, maybe means no, and I don't know means no." When Coach Cal would say this to the team everyone would look around at each other and just laugh. Coach even laughed at himself sometimes when he would say it. He would also say "If a girl hits you, put your hands in your pocket and run away as fast as you can." Even though we found humor in Coach Cal's philosophies, we took him seriously. He has been in the coaching business a long time and has seen everything imaginable happen when it comes to females and athletes. The most popular lesson that Coach would mention was for us to stay away from females who were out to cause drama between teammates. He explained how one female would have relations with two friends on the same team and cause teammates not to like each other. Throughout my previous three years in college I had seen this happen several times, so I understood why

Coach was harping about it.

Coach Cal's meetings involved many topics and lessons other than girl advice. Coach talked to our team about everything. I looked forward to the meetings before practice every day. I've never been so motivated by a person in my life. Whatever I had going on in my world or things that I had running through my mind were all irrelevant when I heard Coach talk. My eyes were glued to him and my ears were open to listen to every message he had to offer. I can remember one particular meeting when he spoke to the team about Derrick Rose signing his new NBA contract and shoe deal. He explained to the team how hard Derrick had worked while he was at Memphis and that all the success that Derrick was having was a result of his hard work. Derrick had just signed a multi-million-dollar shoe endorsement deal and the next day he was in the gym working out. Coach Cal said that nine out of ten people in the room that day would have signed that contract and then sat back on the couch, popped Cheetos, and watched movies all night. By some of my teammate's reactions, no one seemed to disagree. Derrick was a different dude. He still was not satisfied. I sat there in my seat thinking, "If I could sign a deal for that much money, I probably would sit back and pop Cheetos too." I mean, that's a lot of money. For someone who has come from so little you would think that a person would want to celebrate for earning that much money. Derrick and Coach Cal had a different mentality. That is why Coach drove our team and me as an individual to another level. He wanted everyone in the room to make it, regardless if the NBA was your destination or if you were heading towards getting your college degree. Failure was not an option for any of Coach's players. Coach just wouldn't let that happen. If any member of our team did not have that drive, then we would have to move on without them.

All the hard work paid off early in the season. Our first couple of games we basically competed against ourselves. The teams we played were heavily unmatched and Coach Cal challenged the team to keep competing no matter what the score was. Everyone was sharing the ball and everyone was pitching in their fair share of points. You could see that dog mentality in our team that coaches love. Some games early in the season were blowouts and guys were still diving on the floor for loose balls and making hustle plays. Sitting on the sideline in street clothes during home games was no fun at all, but I made the best of it and used every game as an opportunity to learn. Every game I would pay attention to the conversations Coach would have with players on the sideline. I would try my best to grasp the talks that he would have with the team during timeouts. When I became eligible I needed to be well prepared and have an understanding of what Coach was like during games.

As much success as our team had in our first couple of games, there was still room for improvement. Some guys still had not fully bought into the system, but that was ok for now because of how well everyone had been playing together.

Coach Cal preached every day that for us to win a championship everyone must buy in and be on the same page. It wasn't that this was a problem at the time, it was just some players were the best players on their high school team and were used to shooting 40 shots a game. When you're mixed and matched with other great players you're not going to get that many shots every game so you have to be able to adjust.

One night in the dorm I decided to turn on the TV. I turned to ESPN and saw that North Carolina, who was the number one team in the country, was getting beat. I ran up to the lounge area to see if anyone else was watching, and there sat some of my teammates locked into the TV. North Carolina went on to lose that game. After the game was over, we looked around at each other and knew what everyone was thinking. I could remember Kidd-Gilchrist saying, "You know what that means, boys? Number one in the country, baby!"

Everyone else in the room showed some excitement. I sat there and just held my emotions to myself and thought "Number one in the country? I wonder what that would be like." The rankings hadn't even changed yet and people were texting my phone saying, "Congratulations, everyone doesn't get an opportunity to be on the number one team in the country." My whole mentality was "wait, people, the rankings haven't changed yet."

When I got out of class on Monday morning, I walked back to the dorm to take a nap before practice. Usually before my naps I watch a little ESPN just to catch up on sports for the day. The ESPN alert ticker read "UK new number one team in the country." I got so excited I had to cancel my nap plans. I ran down to Anthony's room where he and Darius sat talking about it.

In the meeting before practice that day Coach Cal mentioned it, but reminded us not to be content. Rankings don't mean anything. Now the target on our back had become much bigger, but we are Kentucky and the target on our back is always big.

Being on the number one team in the country was special to me. All my dreams of being a Wildcat and my experiences as a Wildcat were greater than I had ever imagined. It was one thing for me to get the opportunity to be a part of this program and now having the opportunity to be a part of the number one team in the country was huge.

Our biggest game of the season up until this point came against the fifth ranked North Carolina Tar Heels. All the preseason trash talk about which team was the favorite to win the national championship was between UK and UNC. This was setting up to be a game for the ages. Eleven potential NBA players were going to be featured in this game. We were ready. We wanted to go out and prove to the world that we were the best team in the country.

After a good hard week of practice, it was show time. All week we heard rumors about different celebrities who were going to attend this game. Someone mentioned Drake being in attendance, but I wasn't going to believe that until I saw it.

Walking into Rupp Arena there stood John Wall and DeMarcus Cousins who were wishing everybody on the team good luck before walking into the locker room. When the team ran out for warm ups, the arena was already packed and electric. I just sat there and thought, "Wow! This is why I wanted to come to UK, to be a part of games like this." I leaned over to one of the coaches during warm ups and said, "This atmosphere is crazy. I've never seen anything like it." As we were lining up to do team introductions, I saw a 6'8'' guy that I thought looked very familiar come sit behind our bench. From where I was standing in the introduction line I couldn't really get a good look at him. When we went to sit down on the bench before tipoff, one of my teammates tapped me and said, "Dude, do you see Tracy McGrady sitting behind us?" I turned all the way around in my seat and stared him down for about fifteen seconds. McGrady was my brother's favorite NBA player and I also admired him. He was at the game rooting for us. The only thing that ran through my head was "I wonder if my brother sees him." My brother was sitting with my mom at the other end of the arena so I knew there was probably no chance that he saw him or even knew he was at the game.

Star struck time was over, and luckily I turned my head around just in time to witness Terrence Jones dunking all over one of UNC's players off of a missed free throw. I hopped up out of my seat extremely excited. After the first few minutes of the game, I knew I was going to spend most of this game on my feet cheering. The game went back and forth like a heavy weight fight, both teams coming at each other. This game had me on edge. I wanted to be out there so bad and help my teammates fight a tough battle. All of the back and forth in the game came down to one defensive stop for our team. We were up one point and North Carolina had the ball and an opportunity to take the last shot. All of us on the sideline were hugging each other, praying for one defensive stop. UNC tried to throw the ball into their big man Tyler Zeller. He fumbled the ball and it ended up in the hands of John Henson for what appeared to be an easy ten-foot jump shot. Out of nowhere came Anthony Davis who blocked the shot and saved the game. We recovered the ball and dribbled until the time ran out. Rupp Arena went crazy. Everyone on the team ran to Anthony, jumped on him, and congratulated him. From where I was sitting, there was no doubt in my mind that Henson was going to make that shot if he had gotten it off.

The team was heading out for our second road game of the season to none other than Bloomington, Indiana, to face the Hoosiers. The Hoosiers had been through a tough stretch the past couple of years, but Coach Tom Crean had revived the program and Coach Cal knew that it would not be an easy game for us. Once again, I had to stay in Lexington, but I said my prayers with the team as they headed out. Not too long after the team left, I received a call from one of my high school teammate's mom, Mrs. Pam Gowers. She informed me that she was going to be cooking steaks for the game the next evening and wanted to know if I wanted to join them. With no hesitation I accepted. Throughout my high school career, Mrs. Gowers would always have the team over for dinner and I always loved when she made steaks. That evening I arrived at Mrs. Gowers' house about an hour before game time. My brother and my friend Eddie were also invited by Mrs. Gowers so they just rode with me.

When we arrived at the Gowers' house, dinner was already prepared and all we had to do was sit down, pick up the knife and fork, and begin to eat. The whole time we were eating everyone at the table kept making predictions about the game. Everyone thought it would be tough to beat Indiana at Indiana, but of course I had the confidence in my team and thought that we would take care of Indiana easily. Mrs. Gowers got up from the table and went into the TV room to turn the TV on. Dick Vitale's voice filled the house. I yelled at everyone at the table, "It's game time, boys!"

We quickly got up from the table, walked into the TV room, and took our positions on the couch. There were a lot of good and bad things that happened during that game, but the only thing that I remember was the last play. Indiana had the ball with six seconds left and was down two. I couldn't even watch the last six seconds because I just had a feeling that Indiana was going to make a desperation shot. I got up off the couch, sat on the floor, and closed my eyes before Indiana inbounded the ball. I heard my brothers and even Mrs. Gowers yelling and screaming at the TV as Indiana was pushing the ball up the court. Then out of nowhere, complete silence. I raised my head and said, "Did he make it?" but before I even got the question out I saw that Indiana players and fans had already rushed the court and were celebrating.

I could see some of my teammates scattered throughout the mayhem. I felt so bad for my brothers. I just sat there with my hands over my head thinking that this could not be real. Mrs. Gowers, probably one of the biggest Kentucky fans that I know, had tears in her eyes. One thing I did know from knowing my teammates was that it would be harder for someone to beat us again because we would bring it every day in practice to make sure it didn't happen.

That next week of practice was hell. Quickly we got a taste of what Coach Cal was like after a loss, and it wasn't good. He got after some guys like he had never got after them before. He was getting in guys' faces, and he was calling guys out for things that he had let go previously. Practices were physical and like a war. If you weren't competitive there was no way you could even walk in the gym that week. I mean I didn't even travel with the team to Indiana and I was even getting havoc. It was a tough week for me. I had to match up with the toughest and meanest player on our team throughout that week of practice, Kidd-Gilchrist. Kidd-Gilchrist turned it up another level. He was guarding me in practice like I stole something from him. I didn't back down one bit. I brought the competitiveness right back at him and we both got better that week.

Other guys were competing hard as well. Terrence Jones and Kyle Wiltjer had a few scuffles, Eloy Vargas and Kidd-Gilchrist shared a few unpleasant words, and I even had a few run-ins with Marquis Teague. It wasn't about anyone on the team not liking each other, it was just that as a team we had to up the intensity and push each other to another level. Some guys on the team clearly made it a point that we would not lose again for the rest of the season and I believed them. After the Indiana loss we got on a roll and never looked back. We were beating teams easily and having a lot of fun while doing it. We would be blowing teams out and Coach Cal would never let the team relax for one possession. In timeouts he always reminded the team to not look at the score and to compete every possession because that's what we would have to do in the national championship game. It didn't matter if we slipped up and lost a game or not to our coaching staff, as long as we fought hard, played together, and got better. Our team was so talented and if we improved each and every week there would be no way any team could beat us by the end of the year.

Time was getting closer and closer. My eligibility restrictions were coming to an end. Everyone in my family was getting anxious. When I would be out in public somewhere fans would come up to me and say things like "Good luck when you become eligible", "Hope you get some playing time" and stuff of that nature. Most people had the idea that I was going to get some back up playing time at point guard. I had been playing all kinds of positions in practice. I was just hoping that whenever I became eligible I would get some playing time. I didn't care what position. I would play center if I needed to. I just wanted to be out there playing in a Kentucky uniform. I wanted to be out there playing with my brothers because they looked like they'd been having so much fun.

My teammates used to mess with me about finally getting back on the court. Some of them used to play little jokes and tell me that I was the missing piece or say that they could not wait to play with me. Even though I wasn't suiting up, I still felt like I was a big part of everything, which helped me get over the fact that I wasn't playing. I used to get down on myself a lot because I couldn't travel with the team or participate in certain things, but my teammates made sure to always keep me a part of what they could.

All of the waiting and anticipation finally ended. December 17th was here. It was time for me to suit up and be a part of this great team that we were building. The University of Chattanooga was in town and not a better game could have been scheduled for me to return. The head coach of Chattanooga, John Shulman, recruited me the hardest when I was coming out of high school. I took a visit to Chattanooga and fell in love with Coach Shulman. He was such a nice guy and appeared to be a pretty good coach from what I saw. It was hard to turn down Chattanooga because of how hard they recruited me. Coach Shulman also recruited me a little bit while I was in prep school and even recruited me a little bit during my transfer process. I imagined that when I checked into the game against them that he would have a big smile and no animosity toward me because he knew everything I had gone through to get to this point in my career.

On my way to the game I was as hyped as I had ever been. I dressed extra fancy. I wanted to portray a professional look so I wore nice slacks and a nice collared shirt. Earlier that day I had gone and gotten my car washed. If you had asked me, I would have told you that I was preparing myself for this big-time return.

When I walked into the arena, the entire faculty and administrators wished me good luck. I immediately started getting nervous as I was walking into the locker room. All the talking and dreaming about being a UK basketball player was over; it was time to finally be one and show the Big Blue Nation that I belonged.

To make a long story short, my night did not go as planned. I sat over on the bench forever and ever waiting to get in the game. We were up big the majority of the second half so I thought I could get my name called at any time. That was not the case. I kept waiting and waiting. I even looked at Coach Cal a few times to see if he was looking down toward me on the bench. I was hoping to make eye contact with him, which also failed.

The second half was winding down and the fans were

leaving and heading toward the exits. I was mad and frustrated. It was impossible to not express it on my face. Fans started yelling "Put Twany in the game!" That didn't bother me at all. It actually made me realize that people cared about me and wanted to see me get in and do well. There were about three minutes left on the clock and Coach Cal signaled for me to go in. I wasn't even excited anymore, but I was happy to finally get on the court for the first time. I checked into the game and the fans that were still there gave me a nice ovation. That immediately put a smile on my face, but my heart was beating pretty fast. I just thought, "What can I do in these three minutes to stand out?"

The game was a little out of reach and at this point both teams were basically walking the ball up and down the court. Whenever the guy I was guarding got the ball I tried to play intense defense, but it was a little too late in the game. No one else was playing hard. I didn't even break a sweat. The buzzer sounded and the game was over. I was furious, but in no way, shape, or form could I show this to my teammates, the coaches, or the fans. I so badly wanted to show my teammates that I was ready to play, but I guess this game wasn't meant for me to do that.

When we were shaking hands with the other team, I grabbed Coach Shulman and gave him a big hug and he looked at me and said, "You are supposed to be my point guard." I just smiled at Coach Shulman and wished him good luck on the rest of the season.

After the game, I stayed at Rupp Arena about an extra hour than I normally do discussing matters with my family. My mom didn't like the look I had on my face when I checked into the game and she felt like I needed to apologize to my coach. My cousin Kevin was mad at me for not dominating the game in the three minutes that I was given. I kept making excuses that I should have played more and expressed how upset I was. My mom kept reminding me that this was an incredible opportunity and to not blow it by being selfish. I eventually stopped trying to fight it and agreed with what my family was saying.

My big day wound down. I didn't get the results I had planned for, but immediately I learned a lesson. It made me realize that nothing is given and that I had to continue to work hard.

The next two weeks went by really fast, and before I knew it Louisville was up next on the schedule. If you knew me, then you knew that there was not a team on the schedule that I dreamed of playing against more than Louisville. Even though I am from Louisville, I have always been a diehard Kentucky fan. The U of L and UK rivalry has always been something that I looked forward to each and every year as a fan and now I had the opportunity to be a part of this rivalry. I remember when I was young and watching the UK – U of L game one time, Derek Anderson went baseline and dunked all over a U of L player and I went crazy. One, because I knew him, and two, because he was from Louisville and was ballin' at Kentucky. I used to dream that I could make a play like that one day in that type of a rivalry game. A few years later Rondo, who was also a Louisville native playing for Kentucky, had one of his best games of his college career versus Louisville in Freedom Hall. Derek and Rondo inspired people like me to have that dream of playing in this rivalry game and performing very well.

The week of practice leading up to the Louisville game was very intense. Coach Cal tried to get us ready for a war. The way Louisville plays is very rugged and we had to be ready for it. If not, they could run us out of the gym. All week during drills we focused on playing through bumps and hard fouls because that was just how Louisville played. Practice was a lot of fun because I was one of the guys who Coach Cal assigned to foul and hack everyone else in practice. Nobody had a problem with it; we were just preparing for the game.

I was really emotional that week. I knew everybody in the state would be watching this game and especially people from Louisville that knew me. I wanted so badly to get into the game and contribute any way possible. Ticket requests that week were crazy. I got so many calls for tickets for that game, but I only had 4 tickets. When it all boiled down to it, I was just hoping that we won the game against Louisville. If we were to lose, I wouldn't hear the last of it from people when I went back home.

Running out onto the court for warm-ups, Rupp Arena was electric. I could tell from warm-ups that this game was going to have the same electricity as the North Carolina game. We were lining up for the National Anthem and as usual I was looking up at the flag singing the anthem to myself. When the anthem was over, we were taking our positions for the starting line ups. Out of nowhere I heard this big roar from the crowd. I immediately turned around to see what was going on, and my mouth just dropped. There standing courtside was Jay Z. I don't get star struck much, but Jay Z got me. All I kept looking at was how big and shiny his chain was. After the introductions I sat down on the bench and just thought, "Man, we have Jay Z at our game; this is incredible!" During the game he was one of our biggest fans. One would have thought he was an alumnus. When certain plays were made, he was up fist pumping and clapping.

The game was going as well as advertised. Both teams were playing really hard. It was a war just like Coach Cal had prepared us for. There were about three minutes left in the first half and one of our guards picked up his second foul. Coach Cal looked down the bench, paused a second, and then called my number. I hopped up off the bench and ran to the scorer's table. I looked around and couldn't believe I was checking into a UK - U of L game and about to play in front of arguably the greatest rapper of all time. It surprised me that when I checked into the game, I wasn't even nervous. I was assigned to guard Russ Smith, which was a tough task and it showed on my first defensive possession. I played great defense on Russ Smith, but he threw up an acrobatic shot that went in.

On offense I wanted to get up a shot so bad, but I never really got to touch the ball. On one possession I cut backdoor and got a pass from Darius Miller. I threw a pass around Gorgui Dieng to Kyle Wiltjer for an easy layup. I got hyped. Louisville was making a run and my play put a stop to their run and changed the momentum. Running back down the court I peeped over to Jay Z to see if he was looking.

The end of the half came quicker than I wanted it to. Coach Cal was right about how Louisville grabbed and fouled the whole game, so the adjustments at half time were to keep being strong with the ball because we knew they were going to pick up their defensive aggressiveness. In the second half we didn't have a problem. We took care of the ball and cruised safely to a very hard-earned victory. I didn't play at all in the second half, but I was still happy that we got the win.

After the game, all my friends and family were calling me hyped about the game and were all happy to see me get in. One of my best friends, Jazz, was mad at me because I didn't take about five shots. I had to tell Jazz that taking shots was not my job, but he was just messing around with me.

Now that the Louisville game was over and out of the way, it was time to refocus on the bigger goal. Our winning streak continued and the season was going by so fast. I guess when you're winning and having fun, you don't realize how fast it is going. That's what makes being on a team like this so special. Everything that we went through, we had to appreciate it and take advantage of all the opportunities because my teammates and I could possibly never be on a team like this again. Coach Cal stressed this to us all season. There were several guys on the team that we all knew would be going to the NBA after the season. Coach Cal always told us to be thankful for what you have now because on the next level things will be different. The NBA was a profession and it's all about money. Not all teams have that team cohesion like we did on this team. For the most part, that message got through to my team and we cherished every moment together.

Here we were on the road at Florida with an opportunity to go 16-0 in conference play and win the SEC regular season. It was Florida's senior night and we wanted to spoil it for them. Florida's crowd was loud and electric. We put a control on that immediately. We came out of the gates firing. Terrence Jones started the game like a mad man. Terrence knew that their four man couldn't guard him, so he came out aggressive early and got us off to a good start. Florida never really threatened us that game. We were hitting on all cylinders and played a very good game overall. For it being such a big win and us winning the SEC regular season, our emotions didn't show it. We not only expected to win the SEC regular season, we expected to win the NCAA Championship. This team never settled and was never satisfied. In the locker room after the game Coach Cal congratulated us, but also reminded us that we had a lot more work that needed to be done.

We went into the SEC Tournament with the number one overall seed and all fingers pointing toward us to bring home the tournament championship. With this conference tournament, we just wanted to continue to get better and prepare ourselves for the NCAA Tournament. Coach Cal prepared us for this tournament like he had prepared us all season. To him winning this tournament really didn't mean anything, but he wanted to see us use this tournament as preparation for the NCAA Tournament.

With the overall number one seed, we were granted a first round bye and opened the second round with LSU. With it being our first game and LSU's second game, it gave all of the advantage to LSU. They had already played a game the previous day and were accustomed to the arena and the rims. This showed at the beginning of the game. They played us really close and hung with us for half of the game. LSU played like they had nothing to lose and gave us a really good test. We needed it though. We needed to be physically and mentally challenged.

We advanced to the conference semi-finals where we faced Florida. All everyone in the media kept saying was that it would be hard to beat this Florida team three times in one season. We weren't trying to buy into that myth. We just wanted to go out and play. As people predicted, Florida played us really close. They made a bunch of tough shots, but we did too. I remember the game being neck and neck until midway through the second half when Kidd-Gilchrist empowered his will on the game. We were struggling to find points late in the game and Kidd-Gilchrist went and got a couple of tough rebounds and put backs that were huge. Only a mad man could have got those rebounds. He willed us to a tough earned victory. That 'playing-a-team-three-times' myth almost got us, but we prevailed.

Darius Miller had struggled the past two games and to win the NCAA championship we needed our senior leader to have a big impact. Before the championship game tipped off, Kidd-Gilchrist, who was starting at small forward, went to Coach Cal and pleaded for Darius Miller to start in his place. Kidd-Gilchrist basically stated to him that for us to win in the big tournament we need Darius to play well. So, when Coach called the starting line ups in the locker room before the game and Darius was in the lineup, everyone looked around the room confused because no one knew that Kidd-Gilchrist had gone to Coach Cal.

The playing-a-team-three-times myth was haunting us again. This was going to be the third time that we had faced a very good Vanderbilt team this season. The game went back and forth the whole game. Big play after big play. Darius Miller starting paid off completely. He was back to playing like himself. He was back to making the big plays that we had seen him make all year. We had all the momentum going into the under-four-minute time out. I was hoping that we could close out these four minutes and be crowned SEC Tournament Champions again. My freshman year at Mississippi State I had the opportunity to win an SEC Championship. Last year during my transfer year at UK we won the SEC Championship in Atlanta, and now that I was on the sidelines I wanted to experience the feeling of winning an SEC Tournament again with my team and the rest of the Big Blue Nation.

Out of the timeout Vanderbilt made a couple shots, got a few stops, and the momentum of the game totally changed. They took full control of the game and we couldn't make enough plays to get over the hurdle. All I could remember was sitting in a silent locker room and listening to Vanderbilt's team celebrate like they had won a national championship.

I've lost a lot of games in my life, but it was something about that loss that was different than any other loss. Everyone in the room looked sick to their stomach. My teammates were crying. I usually don't show that much emotion or cry in front of other people, but I was even crying. If a person didn't know any better they would have thought our season had just ended. I thought Coach Cal would be mad when he came in to the locker room after the game, but he was all positive. If we were going to lose anytime Coach Cal was glad we lost in the conference tournament. He thought we needed a loss. Coach Cal was really big on seeing how guys would respond. And with the guys in our locker room I'm pretty sure Coach Cal knew the type of response that he would get out of us. We had warriors. There was no doubt in my mind that we were going to take this loss and learn from it and be ready to go come NCAA Tournament time. He reminded us to focus on the bigger picture and that it was time to get back to Kentucky and perfect our craft. After we huddled up as a team, Kidd-Gilchrist being who he is, reminded everybody that we would not lose again. Every player nodded their head in agreement.

The championship game ended a few hours before the selection show began. Coach took a vote of people who wanted to stay there in New Orleans and watch it at the arena and people who wanted to get on the plane and head back to Kentucky. The majority wanted to get on the plane and head back. Coach Cal had the selection show recorded for us to watch when we got back home. When we landed at the airport in Lexington, our fans surrounded the gate to welcome us home. Most of us were surprised that the fans showed up even after a loss, but that's why we have the best fans in the world. They support us whether we win or lose. We went over to the fences and interacted with the fans and thanked them for being there and then got on the bus and headed toward Coach Cal's house to watch the recorded selection show.

When we walked into Coach Cal's house, there may have been 100 cameras, all news media. The mood of our team was still affected by the loss. As expected, we received the number one overall seed of the NCAA Tournament and were very pleased and thankful to be rewarded for our hard work all season. Once again, this was another first in my career. It's an honor to be able to play in the NCAA Tournament, but to be the number one overall seed was amazing. We were all happy that we got the number one seed because we would be able to play in Louisville for the first two rounds, so the first two games would essentially be home games for us. This marked the beginning of a new six-game season, and going 6-0 meant we would be National Champions.

***

Chapter 12:
THE BIG EASY

The plane landed safely in New Orleans. We were back but this time we were here to claim our national championship. The feeling that we had leaving New Orleans a few weeks ago still left a bad taste in our mouths, and there was no way we were leaving with that taste again. We were hungry, humbled, and more focused. We were ready for our moment. What a place for the Final Four to be held. The Big Easy was ready for some great basketball. Riding through the town headed toward our hotel we thought we were in Lexington, Kentucky. Our fans literally painted the town blue. Wildcat fans were standing out in the streets, sitting at the bars, flooding the restaurant, and filling up hotel lobbies. They were simply everywhere! It was amazing to see all the Kentucky fans that had traveled all the way down to New Orleans to support us and our mission of winning the schools eighth national championship. It took a minute or two for everything to sink in. I always look at each situation and take time out to picture everything and realize what a great opportunity I was experiencing. This whole feeling still seemed so surreal. Whenever I reminisce, I always come to the fact that I had this dream my whole life and I was able to live it. Dreams do come true. I know some basketball players' dreams are to reach the NBA and for the most part mine was too, but putting on that Kentucky uniform and reaching the Final Four was also a dream of mine. We were one game away from playing for the national championship. Our season up until this point had been tremendous, but anything less than holding up that trophy Monday night would have been a failure.

Every team that made it to this point in the tournament was a great team and we knew that each game was going to be difficult. Kansas was rolling at the time, Ohio State was a physical team, and in our first game we had to face the swarming defense of the Louisville Cardinals. Being matched up with Louisville scared me the most. It had nothing to do with the talent. but everything to do with the toughness Louisville played with and the deep rivalry that existed between UK and Louisville. Whenever Louisville gets to pressing and scoring easy buckets off of their defense they are really hard to beat. Louisville was coming into the Final Four as one of the hottest teams in the country. If we lost to our in-state rival it would be much harder on our fans than if we lost to any other team. The loss would be close to home and amplified. We would never hear the end of it. However, it was a great opportunity for the whole state of Kentucky to come together for something positive. Louisville and UK both in the Final Four was huge for the state because of all of the publicity it attracted.

We were well prepared for any situation that was going to be in front of us. In the second round of the tournament we were challenged by a tough Iowa State team. In the Sweet Sixteen we had a chance to redeem ourselves against Indiana who had given us our first loss of the season. Baylor, who had several future NBA players on their team, was a great test and our team proved to the country that game that we were going to be a force to be reckoned with.

We cut the nets down as regional champions in Atlanta, put the hats on, smiled, and hugged for the cameras. However, we made sure not to over celebrate because we had much bigger goals in mind. We had one more net we wanted to cut down and another hat we wanted to put on. My mom, who has rarely traveled out of the state of Kentucky, teamed up with a few family members of mine and made the trip to New Orleans. Seeing her in New Orleans might have been the highlight of my trip. All the parents on our team were extremely close so my mom got to hang out with some of my other teammates' parents. She walked Bourbon Street and partied at every possible opportunity. This was big for her. She was getting to see a whole new life outside of Louisville,

Kentucky. I knew Mom was caught up in the moment when she started talking about wanting to live in New Orleans after only being there for two days. My brother was even telling me that it was hard to keep Mom in the room and that she was hardly getting any sleep. I had no problem with it as long as she was having fun and enjoying life. We just let her be.

As a team, we rarely went out. We wanted to remain focused on the task at hand. Besides maybe grabbing some food with our families, we pretty much stayed together as a team. We practiced several times at Tulane University's facilities. Practices were not really built around much contact, but more so being crisp and going over our game plans. We still went hard, but contact was minimal to avoid injury and to keep us fresh. Our practices were maybe an hour or a little bit over. We got on the practice court, went as hard as Coach Cal wanted us to, and were off the court in no time.

After two days of practicing at Tulane University we were given the opportunity to practice in the Super Dome. My anticipation to step foot in the Super Dome was at an all-time high because I looked at it in a different perspective than everybody else. I was thinking, "Dang! I'm walking in the same place Drew Brees and many other NFL players have walked in and had many memorable games." I always looked at things differently and appreciated things differently than everybody else.

As soon as we got past the curtains and were making our way onto the floor, I just stopped and looked up like

"Wow!" I wondered if the depth perception would have any impact on the way we shot the ball. You talk about being jacked up for a practice, I was ecstatic. I could look up, and up, and up for days. I pulled out my cell phone and just took pictures of what I was seeing.

While we were supposed to be getting ready for practice I was sightseeing. My teammates will always remember Twany Beckham's first shot in the Super Dome. My teammates and I had this routine that whenever we all go onto the court for the first time we all watch each other's first shot attempt. It's funny because everyone isn't warmed up and usually it takes someone to attempt a couple shots before they get comfortable with the rim. Nine times out of ten our first shot is not a good one. I was too hyped and anxious and wanted to take the first shot and it backfired on me. From the top of the key I attempted a three-pointer and the ball went far left. It hit the bottom pad on the left side of the backboard. I knew as soon as the ball left my hands that it was not a good shot. When the ball hit the backboard all of my teammates just fell out and started laughing at me. I didn't get mad at them for laughing at me; it was actually funny. I wasn't afraid to step up and take the first shot. I'm not going to call anyone out, but there were some shots after mine that were just as bad. I'm not really sure who started this routine, but it was something we started on the road early in the season and it stuck with us.

We had been down in New Orleans a few days and all week we had been busy with media and Final Four duties. One day we had to go to the Super Dome for video shoots and interviews. The next day all four teams attended a Final Four banquet. The Final Four banquet was very unique. All four teams came together for a nice meal and all the players and coaches were introduced. We were getting anxious to play. We had received all the preparation that we needed from the coaching staff. It was time to go out there and show the world what we came to do.

It was probably ten o'clock the night before we played Louisville and Coach Cal had us in his room for last-minute preparations. Coach wanted to say a few more words to us about having our minds right and going out to perform like champions. He felt like he had done everything to prepare us and that by doing so he could sleep like a baby. He said he wanted us to remain focused and wake up in the morning on the same beat with one goal. When I got back into my room I was full of energy. Maybe it was nervous energy or just pure excitement. Sleep was not going to come easy for me that night. I'm pretty sure it was the same for my teammates. We all had a goal at the beginning of the season to be on the big stage and we were finally here.

Just like the game back in December against Louisville, this game was just as intense. Two teams who hated each other were out there fighting to survive. I was on edge the whole game. Every time it seemed like we were going to pull away, Louisville would make a play to stay in the game. Late in the second half we were in complete control of the game and Louisville made a big-time run that had everyone extremely nervous. Louisville tied the ball game, but Kidd-Gilchrist stepped up and made a few big plays for us. He had two finishes around the basket during Louisville's run that ultimately won us the game. They were toughness plays. One was an offensive rebound and the other was a dunk over their six-foot eleven-inch center, Gorgui Dieng. I looked at Kyle Wiltjer after Kidd-Gilchrist made that play and said "Kyle, I love that dude." We went on to survive against Louisville, and were headed to the National Championship game.

In the locker room after the game "one more win" was all I heard anyone saying to the media. Everyone who called my cell-phone to say congratulations about the win was quickly cut off. One more win was my response to everything. When we got back to the hotel our fans had flooded the lobby and were all chanting "one more win!" as the team walked up the stairs to our rooms. It was an awesome scene. Our hotel lobby had the looks of a mini pep rally. There was Kentucky Blue everywhere and a bunch of our fans screaming at the top of their lungs.

It wasn't until after I took a shower, got in my bed, and saw our team all over ESPN that I actually realized that we were going to play in the National Championship game. It was just hard to believe. It felt too much like a dream. For the next day or so, sleep was not going to enter my mind. All year we lived by the saying "team no sleep" until we won the National Championship. Well, we had one more night to live that life. All throughout that night I went room to room to see what all my teammates were doing and everybody was wide awake. Anxious, hyped, nervous, whatever you want to call it had everybody awake. One thing I reminded all my teammates about was the fact that this was going to be the last game that we were all going to be together as a team, so we needed to make it a good one. It was going on 4 a.m. before I actually jumped into my bed to close my eyes. We had to be up early for a light breakfast and practice.

Practice the next day was all preparation for our opponent, Kansas. There was not a lot of contact, but we focused on coming up with a game plan on how we were going to defend their post play and how we were going to attack them. Earlier in the season we beat Kansas but that didn't mean anything now. Kansas had improved tremendously and was a physical team. This was going to be a tough game for us to win. There was no doubt in my mind that we would be ready.

***

Chapter 13:
BEST NIGHT OF MY LIFE

I woke up, walked over to the window and pulled the curtains wide open. The sun was beaming and downtown New Orleans was filled with blue. I sat down by the window and watched the activity that was going on while reflecting on this whole journey. My roommate, Brian Long, was not too happy when he was awakened by the light coming into the room. Brian finally rose to his feet and walked over to the window near where I was sitting. He glanced outside at the activity and said, "Today is going to be a good day."

I said, "I hope you're right. Tomorrow we should be waking up as National Champions."

That day was treated just like a typical game day. On the schedule there was a light team breakfast followed by a shoot around at the arena. After the shoot around we came back to the hotel, had a good meal, and then got ready to play a championship game. Everything on the schedule went as planned. Shoot around was sharp and the pregame meal was quiet. I could tell everyone was focused. After the meal we got our normal hour and a half of downtime in our rooms before our bus was scheduled to leave for the arena. Usually on game days guys relax and sometimes watch movies. However, that day everyone was up and out in the hallways pacing around and in each other's rooms.

That hour and a half went by extremely slow. When the time came for us to head to the bus, I ran down to my mom's room and gave her a hug along with my brother and cousin. I managed to get out of my mom's room fast enough to catch up with my teammates who were headed to the lobby. When the elevator doors opened on the first floor, our fans started going crazy. Cameras flashed from every angle. "Go Big Blue" chants echoed throughout the lobby. There were so many fans in the lobby that we had a narrow path from the elevator to the bus. To get through, we had to walk one by one in a single file line. We were all high fiving the fans as we made our way to the door. Our bus was completely blocked in by our fans. Security had to move people out of the way for us to get onto the bus.

The bus ride was really quiet. It was probably the quietest it had been all year, just like the pregame meal. There was not one person on the team who did not have headphones in listening to their music. The ride over to the arena was short. Everyone went into the locker room and got dressed pretty quickly and wasted no time getting on the floor for warm ups. Everything leading up to the game was the same, except the stakes for this game were much higher.

While we were warming up on the floor and stretching, Celebrities were filing into the arena. I saw Samuel L. Jackson, Shaquille O'Neal, and none other than Jay Z, whose seats were right behind our bench.

We ran into the locker room for the last time before tipoff and sat patiently waiting for Coach to give us our final pep talk. As I looked around the room I saw guys sweating which let me know that we had a good warm up. I expected for Coach to come in the locker room and give us a long speech, but I was wrong. Coach appeared to be more relaxed than I had ever seen him before, and if he wasn't he did a great job of acting like it. He simply told our team that if we go out and ball like he knew we could, then we should be fine. Coach didn't really have to say much to fire our team up. He knew how bad each and every member of the team wanted to win this game and that he did not have to use a pregame speech to convince anyone to go out there and play their hardest.

We came out hitting on all cylinders. We jumped out on Kansas and held a comfortable lead for most of the game. This was the most hyped the bench had been all year. We stood up on every play. I prayed during this game about 100 times. You talk about being nervous; I had never been that nervous in my entire life. Every time we took a shot I wanted it to go in. When we got a comfortable lead on Kansas I was hoping we could blow them out because my nerves could not handle a close game. However, basketball is a game of runs and I knew that it was only a matter of time before Kansas made their run and put some pressure on us. We held a double-digit lead for most of the second half, but the basketball gods had to put their imprint on the game. Kansas started making shots that they were not making in the first half, which allowed them to get back into the game. My heart and mind were racing. I thought I was going to have a heart attack when Kansas went on their run.

It was late in the game and Kansas had the ball coming out of a timeout. We were up six and needed another solid defensive stop to secure the game. In the timeout Coach Cal specifically told Kidd-Gilchrist that Kansas would be running a backdoor on his side and to stay alert. Coach was exactly right. Kansas brought the ball down the court and ran a back door play to Kidd-Gilchrist's side. Kidd-Gilchrist must have forgotten what Coach Cal said to him in the timeout and got caught sleeping on the wing. The guy Kidd-Gilchrist was guarding had beaten him so bad anyone watching the game would have thought that Kansas had a free layup. I could see it from where I was sitting on the bench. When I saw the guy go backdoor I put my hands on my head and said, "Ohhh noo!" Kidd-Gilchrist being who he is somehow caught up with his man and blocked the shot from the other side of the rim. Everyone on the sidelines went crazy. I sat down in my seat and thanked the Lord. I don't believe any other player in the country could have made that play.

Next thing I remember was looking up at the clock and watching it count down from ten as slow as it could possibly move. Teague was dribbling the ball up the court celebrating and everyone on the sidelines was waiting to storm the court. When the clock reached zero I blacked out completely. The last thing I remember was jumping on Kyle Wiltjer's back and the fireworks going off that sounded like shotguns.

This was the second time in a two-week span that our team was cutting down the nets. This time climbing up that ladder seemed a lot sweeter. We were National Champions and we deserved our moment. When I cut my piece of net off the rim I looked toward the crowd to where our families were sitting and saw my mom with a huge smile on her face. I pointed the net towards her and she put both of her hands in the air. To me it looked like she was thanking God for this moment. I could not explain my emotions even if I wanted to. Throughout all the hardships, injuries, and transferring obstacles I finally felt like I was on top of the world standing on that ladder.

I made sure I gave every person on the team a hug and thanked them for a great ride. Without each of my teammates going through what we went through that year as a team, none of this would have been possible. The sacrifices each person on our team had to make in order for our team to reach its potential truly made this moment special. When we got in the locker room we finally got to see Coach Cal have some fun. The whole team rallied around him and we started doing our pregame dance. Coach got in the center and started dancing along with us. The locker room lit up. To see Coach dance in the locker room meant so much to our team and everyone inside the locker room. Coach Cal is usually serious and focused. To see him let loose was special because it made me realize that we had helped him achieve a goal of his own and we allowed him to finally be able to relax and enjoy all the hard work he had put in.

It was all fun at first, but when I got to thinking about that being our last game on the court together with these particular teammates, the moment became bittersweet. There was no way possible that I could imagine being on another team like this. We defined the true definition of brothers. To capture the moment, everyone started gathering together for pictures in the locker room with the trophy.

To cap off the night, the hotel we were staying at had the whole second floor sectioned off for players, coaches, and our families. There was a meal that we could have in the ball room and they had a balcony roped off for all the players. On the balcony there were thousands of Final Four beads that they allowed us to throw off to the enormous crowd of UK fans down below. I got to bring my mom, my brothers, my cousins, and some of my friends onto the balcony with me to throw beads. Some of my friends were thanking me for including them in the celebrations and making this the night of their lives as well. We stood out on the balcony and threw beads for several hours. It was truly a night to remember. What made me the happiest was that my mom got to experience everything with me. My mom means so much to me. To see her finally getting to enjoy herself for a week without any worries or stressing over bills made me really happy. I still have a long life to live, but I'm not sure if any night can ever top that one.

***

Chapter 14:
GEEK OF THE YEAR

Life was good during this time of the year. The semester was coming to an end, Derby weekend was coming up, and we were heading to the White House to meet President Obama. Two weeks before we were set to leave, our staff had everyone on the team fitted for their own personalized suit. I was excited, especially because this was going to be the first suit that I had ever owned. Our suits came in two days before we were scheduled to leave. I tried my suit on and loved the way it fit. There was only one problem; I was going to need help with my tie. I had never worn a tie so I had no clue how to tie one.

On the day we were leaving I had one final exam to take that morning and after that I was finished with classes.

After my final exam, I rushed back to my room and got dressed quickly to get on the bus. Everyone on the team was all dressed up and looking fancy. We were all excited about meeting the President.

As we got off the plane in Washington, D.C., I was trying to make a decision on whether to take my backpack with me on the bus or leave it on the plane. Ryan Harrow, who was sitting in the seat next to me, saw me debating with myself and told me to leave my backpack on the plane. With no hesitation I took my backpack off my back, threw it in the seat, and exited the plane. It did not cross my mind at all that my wallet with my identification card was in my backpack. With traffic it took us about an hour to get from the airport to the White House. When we arrived at the White House security got on our bus and started asking everyone for their identification cards. When they got to where I was sitting I reached in my back pockets for my wallet but felt nothing. I stood up and looked all around me in the seat and on the floor but did not see my wallet. Then all of a sudden, I realized that my wallet was on the plane in my backpack. I looked at the security guard and said, "Sir, I don't have my I.D."

With no hesitation he looked at me and said, "Then you cannot go into the White House" and went on to the next person. The word traveled quickly throughout the bus and everyone was asking me how in the world I left my I.D. on the plane. I had no answers for anyone. I just lowered my head and tried to stop the tears from rolling down my face. I was so embarrassed. Everyone started getting off the bus and I remained seated. I was very frustrated and mad at myself. I thought that I had blown the once-in-a-lifetime opportunity to meet the President. Coach Cal told me that the team had to go on without me but that he would call the airport to see if they could have someone bring my I.D. to me. With D.C. traffic, it could take hours before I saw my I.D.

While the team went on ahead and walked into the White House I was on the bus by myself playing the waiting game. I called my mom to tell her the horrible news. All she kept asking was how I made such a big mistake. The more questions she kept asking, the more frustrated I became. I called Pops and told him the mistake I made and he could not believe it. I just sat there in my seat with my head down thinking, "Why me?"

Forty-five minutes went past and the people bringing my I.D. still had not shown up. Out of nowhere this lady walked onto the bus and told me that they were trying to figure out a way to let me in. After about ten minutes of waiting with the lady, she was given permission to let me into the gates of the White House. I ran as fast as I could through security to try to catch up with everyone else.

As soon as I walked into the doors my teammates were lined up to go into the room where Obama was going to talk. I made into the White House just in time. Two minutes later and I would have missed the whole experience. I got in line right as Obama was walking around the corner and got to shake his hand. Here I was this kid from the Beecher Terrace projects out of Louisville, Kentucky, standing on stage with the President of the United States.

When we got back to the bus everyone had a thousand jokes and gave me the "Geek of the Year Award". The word "geek", which was started by Doron Lamb, refers to when someone does something stupid or messes up. I did not want that award, but it happened to me and I had to accept it.

***

Chapter 15:
DEDICATION

The spring semester ended in early May. The returning players and the incoming freshmen were not due back on campus until early June for summer school. The whole month of May I wanted to focus on conditioning and working on my game. I wanted to come back a much better conditioned athlete then I had ever been. I contacted Corey S. Taylor, who is a personal trainer in Atlanta, Georgia. My friend, Leroy, who worked out with Corey the previous summer said that Corey got him in the best condition he had ever been in. I worked out a way that I could go to Atlanta and train for about two weeks. I was taking the necessary steps to dedicate my senior year to becoming a better player and to hopefully get more playing time. The first week of training with this new trainer went really well. He pushed me to a limit that I did not know I had. The first couple of days I trained with him I almost vomited halfway through the workouts. He was as intense of a trainer as I had ever worked with. I needed this. We never touched a basketball. It was all conditioning and core strengthening. We were even going on top of apartment buildings and doing agility drills and parachute running.

I was as focused as ever. Every day after workouts I went home and had dinner and went to sleep. I didn't tell too many people where I was. I hardly answered my phone. I wanted no distractions. I was determined to get better. After several weeks of working out in Atlanta, I returned home to Louisville to focus on the basketball aspects of my game. I got up every morning to work on my jump shot and ball handling. In the afternoons, I would go play pickup with notable college and NBA players. That became my daily routine. Jump shooting was the weakest part of my game and pickup was the perfect setting to work on this skill. I consistently made shots and people were noticing the improvement. I took advantage of every opportunity I had playing in the same gym as Rondo. From a point guard perspective, I watched how he ran a team and got others involved. From a competitive standpoint, I tried to guard him as much as possible. Rondo competes at a high level and I wanted to up my intensity level. I trained so much the month of May it almost seemed as if I didn't have any time off. The month of June came fast and it was time for summer school.

***

Chapter 16:
LIFE TOOK ANOTHER TURN

All my hard work during the summer had paid off. I was in the best shape of my life and was playing great. With the way I was playing I was expecting more playing time this season. I was so anxious for my senior season to get started. I received my national championship ring that summer and was hungry for another one. This time I wanted to play a bigger role in helping Kentucky win a national championship. However, all of my high hopes were quickly shattered. One morning during preseason I woke up and rolled out of bed and fell to the floor. When I went to stand up, my left leg just gave out. I sat there on the floor for a minute wondering what had just happened. I reached down and touched my leg and it felt numb. I started to panic. I did not know what was wrong with me. I reached over to my computer chair and tried to pull myself up, but struggled. When I rose to my feet a sharp pain ran through my back as if someone was stabbing me. I managed to hobble over to the sink and just looked into the mirror and asked myself "What in the world is going on?"

I had no idea what had caused my leg and my back to act this dysfunctional. We were scheduled to practice in a few hours. I figured whatever was going on with my back and leg would eventually go away after a while. When I got in the locker room for practice the pain had not left, but I showed no frustration at all. I went out on the court for my normal pre-practice routine and something was just not right. I attempted to dunk the ball off of my left leg, but I didn't even get off the ground. My leg gave out. I wanted to tell somebody so bad but I was afraid of people not believing me. I did not know exactly what to say to the trainer. The day before in practice I was perfectly fine, so I thought that telling my trainer the next day that I couldn't feel my legs would have sounded fishy. I was afraid people might think I was just faking an injury to get out of practice, but then again, I came to work every day for the last two years so people should know that I would not fake an injury.

Coach Cal walked into the gym and practice was set to begin. I could not feel my left leg at all and my back was hurting, but I jumped in the first drill anyway. When it was my turn to go in the drill I grabbed the ball, hobbled down the court, and air balled a layup. My left leg was dead. I couldn't jump. Everyone in the gym looked at me like I was crazy. Even after that layup I still didn't say anything. I got back in line and tried to go again and got the same results. Coach Cal yelled at me to pick it up, but I couldn't hide it anymore. I jogged off the court and told the trainer the difficulties I was going through. Just like I expected, he looked at me like I was crazy. I told the trainer that there was no way I could go back into practice with the way my body felt.

I missed about two or three days of practice before I had the chance to go see a doctor. During my doctors visit I had an x-ray and an MRI. My results were scheduled to be back in a few days. At this point I was expecting the worst, but hoping for the best. I got in the cold tub to see if that would bring my leg back to life and I also tried ice and electrical stimulation on my back and legs. Neither one worked.

After about three days our team doctor was scheduled to come in and go over my results with me. While sitting in the doctor's office I was exceptionally nervous. I had a feeling that the news the doctor was getting ready to tell me was not going to be good. I had tried to relieve the pain using various methods, but none of them had worked. I was prepared for the worst, and that's what I got. The doctor told me that I had two bulging disks in my lower back which aggravated the nerves that run down through my left leg. The doctor said that it was not an injury that would keep me from playing, but that it was also an injury that would linger for some time. The doctor and I agreed on trying cortisone shots in my back to see if that would help relieve the pain. If the cortisone shots did not help, then surgery was the next best option.

After the first cortisone shot I felt some relief and returned to practice. About two weeks after that my leg started going numb and my back flared up again. As a result, the doctor issued another cortisone shot. After the second shot, the same thing happened after about two weeks and the doctor issued me a third one. After the third shot, I felt a lot better. However, once again the relief was only temporary. I was back to square one within two weeks after the third shot. Even though I was dealing with so much pain, I did whatever I could not to give up. There were some days in practice when I could barely walk up and down the court but I was still out there competing.

I debated for several weeks with my mom about having surgery on my back and she was not for it at all. She has had back problems in the past and decided not to get surgery. Mom was not comfortable with the doctors cutting in my back. I understood what Mom was saying, but I was the one who was going through this excruciating pain. Every day my teammates always asked me when I was going to be healthy again and I never had an exact date for them. All of them would always tell me that they missed my competitive nature in practice. After many heated discussions, the deliberation process with Mom came to an end. I opted to get surgery. Coach Cal announced it to the team one morning during breakfast and the look on everyone's faces was devastating. That announcement completely took the air out of the room. It wasn't so much about the team losing their best player; it was more about the team losing a fierce competitor, a great teammate, and a senior leader.

That was a sad moment in my life because it was my last go around. Who knew if I would be the same after the surgery? I had already used up a red shirt year while at Mississippi State due to my hip surgeries. I realized that this was it; my basketball career was over.

***

Chapter 17:
HUMBLED

My mom woke me up fifteen minutes before tipoff. My teammates were on the road about to play a tough Ole Miss team in their hostile arena and I was lying on my back still drugged up from surgery earlier that day. I wasn't able to twist my body, bend over, or lift anything over ten pounds for six weeks. Mom adjusted the TV in the living room so that all I had to do was lean my head over and I could catch all the action. I was in a lot of pain, but nothing was going to stop me from watching my teammates play. That game was not the ideal game for me to watch with the condition I was in. It was a back and forth type game and after every big play I was trying to raise myself up and cheer. My mom kept looking over at me telling me, "Boy, you better be careful!" I didn't care much about my back; I wanted to see my teammates win badly.

Nerlens Noel, who that night had one of the best performances I had ever seen, almost made me get off my couch and stand up. Every time Ole Miss had a chance to get back into the game, Nerlens came up with a big-time block. My teammates were able to pull one out at Ole Miss which made my day a whole lot better.

A lot of my teammates contacted me after the game to see how my surgery went and I congratulated them on winning such a big game. It meant a lot to me for them to check on me, especially after winning a tough game on the road. The rest of the season wasn't as uplifting but served an important purpose. Unlike the year before, our team struggled throughout the season and failed to make the NCAA Tournament. It was only a couple months ago that we were the last team standing and now we were one of the disappointing stories of college basketball. It's very easy to look at the way that our season ended in a negative light, but for all of us it was a valuable lesson. We were all humbled by this experience.

The returning players along with the highly talented incoming freshman were expecting to win a national title like the year before. Our fan base also expected it to be that type of season. When the season fell short of expectations, I realized that nothing is given and I had been given another opportunity to learn from adversity.

To be a National Champion takes incredible team unity and a bunch of hard workers on the same page. Our team failed to do that and we got the results we deserved. It was really tough on me to accept ending my career the way it did, but I'm a firm believer that everything happens for a reason. When I was a young kid I was always around my cousin Tywain, but on a rare night that I wasn't with him he was murdered. I still wonder today if it was meant for me to not be with him that night. I always dreamed of playing for the University of Kentucky and those dreams didn't come true right out of high school. I wonder if life was meant for me to attend prep school and Mississippi State before reaching my dream school. The year I became eligible at my dream school, Kentucky won its eighth national championship. The plan God had for me was shaping up to be amazing. Then the following year, which was my senior year, I suffered a back injury that ended my season and career. Out of all people, I wonder why that had to happen to me.

Life took a turn. Besides school work, I had a bunch of free time. I joined a church and put a lot of effort into attending Bible studies frequently. I got really close with Max Appel, who was the minister for our team Bible study. Max managed to always be available whenever any of us needed him for prayer or even talk about anything that was going on in our lives. With Max everything was confidential. I fell in love with learning about the Bible and becoming closer to God. In my past I've attended church off and on, but never consistently. I found myself going weekly and dragging my friends along with me. With my injury and everything else that was going on in my life, I was able to call Max and talk about it. I realized the power and worth of a prayer and how much of an impact prayer can have on a person's life. I was waking up in the mornings and praying before I started my day and at night before I went to bed. It wasn't until then that I owned my first Bible. Everything I ever questioned was all starting to make sense. God already had a plan for me and the next step in life for me was to trust His plan and believe in Him.

When I underwent hip surgery while at Mississippi State, I began to take school more seriously. The chances of basketball being my future career were becoming slimmer. Then when I got to the University of Kentucky and endured more injuries I began to focus on my education even more. Instead of always going out on weekends and living the college life, I would stay in and get as much school work done as possible. Fall term of my senior year I earned a 4.0 GPA, which was the first time ever in my educational career. My mom and family were all elated about the success I was having in the classroom. When all a person knows and grew up around is basketball, the importance of an education can be overlooked. All my life when certain people would tell me to not put all my eggs in one basket, I now understand why.

***

EPILOGUE

My brother Andre is currently working and has a good head on his shoulders. Andre and I have gotten extremely close and he still continues to be my biggest fan. My youngest brother Mark is in the process of getting his life together. The past few months I have noticed a difference in him. Every time I get the opportunity to talk to Mark I overemphasize to him the importance of having God in his life. My cousin Kevin is out of prison and is still pursuing his music career while continuing to be a positive voice in my corner. My cousin Tywain is no longer with me and I think about him all the time. Tywain is in a better place and may his soul rest in peace. My biological father, who has been drug free since 2005, has come into my life and has supported me in any way that he can. It was tough accepting a person who had abandoned my mom and me for so long, but life is not about holding grudges. My dad's first and only time in Rupp Arena was for my senior day and that meant a lot to me and for our relationship. My relationship with the Whitakers has continued to grow over the years. Without their generosity and guidance, I would not be where I am today. Pops will always be that father figure that I never had. As for my mom, she finally chased her dream and has relocated to Florida. She is still the rock of our family. Mom continues to take care of my brothers and me in any way that she can. She still inspires us with her fighter mentality. For our family, life still has its struggles and we will continue to conquer them together. One thing I have realized over the years is that no matter what obstacles or challenges arise, if you're surrounded by people who love and care about you, one can persevere. Trying to make it in life on your own is the harder route. Everyone needs guidance and support from others. There really are people out there that will genuinely care for you and love you unconditionally. My mom did everything in her power to raise a fine young man, but without the help of the Whitakers I would not have grown into the man I am today.

As I got prepared to walk across the stage on graduation day, I thought about how I had always expected the chapter after college to include the NBA. It finally hit me that I will be walking away from the game of basketball. Basketball was the game that I grew to love so much, the game that allowed me the opportunity to go to college, the game that changed my life forever and the game that allowed me to tell my story. Through my two hip surgeries and my back surgery, I have learned that there are things that happen in life that you cannot control. I have also learned to remain positive during those situations. The closer I've become to God, I have realized that everything happens for a reason. I may be walking away from the game of basketball, but I'm walking towards a life filled with opportunity. On May 5th 2013, I walked across that stage as the first person in my family to ever graduate from college. The smile on my mom's face after walking across the stage was priceless. Her baby boy was all grown up and ready for the real world.

I can't say enough about Coach John Calipari. He prepared me in every way imaginable. I was taught the importance of hard work and dedication. I learned how to take responsibility for my own actions. Coach Cal taught me the importance of having toughness and the mentality to overcome all fears.

I conquered adversity. I beat the odds of kids from the projects graduating from college. I am a National Champion, a graduate from the University of Kentucky, but more than anything, a child of God.

"Twany looks out for everybody and wants the best for everybody. He is an intelligent young man who only wants to succeed in life. He was a great teammate. He is so competitive that he pushed every person on the team to be better. He works hard and never takes a day off. As a friend, Twany is the best anybody can have. He looks out for his friends and is always there for them no matter what. He is always going to be my brother."

-Anthony Davis

"Twany is a great person. I knew him before he and I came to UK. We were close friends and had a bond before we got to the University of Kentucky. He was a great teammate and a guy you can always count on."

-Darius Miller

"Twany is a great friend and individual. He and I got super close during our senior season, and we always had two hour long talks at least two times a week about life and other things that brothers talk about. Meeting Twany was great for me and is another life long bond I look forward to having."

-Julius Mays

A special thanks to my mom, Debra Beckham, who has always been the one constant in my life and shown me unconditional love.

9 780615 845968